AGARICUS BLAZEI MURILL
NOTEBOOK

STEPHEN BLACK

THE AGARICUS BLAZEI MURILL NOTEBOOK

Copyright 2003 by Stephen Black
All rights reserved. No Part of this book may be reproduced or transmitted, by any means, electronic or mechanical without written permission from the author.

Stephen Black, PO Box 6566, Toledo, Ohio 43613

ISBN 1-59113-319-X

Library of Congress Cataloguing in Publication Data

Black, Stephen J., 1960-
The Agaricus Blazei Murill Notebook/ Stephen J. Black
Includes bibliographical references
1. Agaricus-therapeutic use—popular works.
2. Alternative medicine, popular works
3. Anticholesteremic agents-popular works
4. Antineoplastic agents-Popular Works
5. Cancer-Popular works
6. Cancer-Diet therapy
7. Cancer-Nutritional aspects
8. Immunological adjuvants—Popular Works.
9. Herbs, therapeutic use-Japan
10. Medicine-popular works
11. Mushrooms-popular works
12. Mushrooms-therapeutic use

Credits

Cover Design Concept
Stephen Black

Assistance
David Bothwell/Hybrid (London, Hong Kong)
Ritsuko Endo
Eric Nelson

Realized by
Emeline Ang

Photo credits
Larry Lough
Gary Shaw
Stephen Black

Pharmacological Information Assistance
Motone Hayakawa
Proofreading: Patrick Desmond, Edward Schweickart

Table of Contents

History, Facts And Goals	13
Agaricus blazei *Murill* In The World Of Mushrooms	19
Agaricus blazei *Murill* In The Wild	22
Agaricus blazei *Murill* As A Food	24
What Does ABM Do In The Body?	31
Who May Benefit From ABM?	34
What Is Beta Glucan?	36
The Immune System	41
The Body, ABM And Cancer	46
Cancer	47
ABM Tea	49
Frequently Asked Questions	50
An Open Letter To Bono, Bill Gates Or Anyone With A Lot Of Faith, Hope And Trust	55
An Open Letter To Doctors	57
An Open Letter To Those Considering ABM For The First Time	61
Miscellaneous Notes	64

The Freeze-dried Agaricus Homepages 66

My Experiences with ABM: Kim Z. J. Wang 80

Glossary 81

Bibliography 95

Index 101

The Agaricus Blazei Murill Notebook

"Never overlook Nature's abundance- especially the unseen"
Chiaki Williams

The information in this book is based on research collected and interviews conducted by the author, as well as his experiences. The following material is presented for information purposes only and should not be construed as medical advice. The reader is strongly advised to check on any health-related issues with a qualified health professional before implementing any intervention and self-diagnosis is not, in any means encouraged.

Companies, interventions and products are mentioned without bias to increase knowledge only, not as a recommendation, promise of a cure, mitigation, prescription or prevention of any medical condition.

The advice and information in this book are believed to be accurate at the time of going to press. However, neither the author, the editors nor the publisher can accept any legal responsibility for any errors or admissions made. The publisher makes no warranty, express or otherwise, with respect to the materials contained within this publication.

Talk about agaricus blazei murill and your health with your doctor.

About the author

Stephen Black is a writer, an artist, a prize-winning photographer and a digital moviemaker. He has worked with CNN, Walker Asia, Fox TV, Cartoon Network, Fuji TV, The Asian Channel and publications including Esquire (Japan), People, South China Morning Post. He is represented as a photographer by nonstock (www.nonstock.com), a New York-based photo agency and represented as an artist by galerie omote-sando in Tokyo.

Black is currently based in New York, Tokyo and Singapore, with frequent trips to the U.S. and Europe. At the time of this writing, he is working on a mushroom documentary as well as a digital feature-length movie in which ABM is barely mentioned.

Notice

The author is the co-founder of the Freeze-Dried Agaricus Blazei *Murill* Center, which promotes the freeze-dried form of ABM and deals exclusively with products supplied by the Taiai Company. The FDABM website can be found at www.freezedriedagaricus.com.
However, every effort towards neutrality has been taken in regards to other forms of ABM, as the author's purpose is to share reliable information as well as increase knowledge and public trust in all matters regarding ABM.

It should also be noted that in Japan, Taiai is considered to be a pioneer in the production of ABM. They are certified by the Japanese government as a producer of food and they are working in conjunction with top university medical researchers. They have licensed their mushroom-growing methods to other companies.

For this author, they represent the standard of quality and occupy a special place in the history of ABM usage in Japan and the world.

Included in this book are pages from the Freezedried Agaricus Blazei *Murill* website, pages interpreted from Japanese and written by the author. Although the pages encourage the use of the freeze-dried form of ABM, the information from the site applies to all forms of ABM. The website is constantly being updated with the latest news regarding all types of ABM and can be found at www.freezedriedagaricus.com.

In regard to this same topic, I would like to point out the freeze-drying technique used by Taiai has been tested by an independent, Japanese government agency to have high levels of beta-glucans and other valuable components.

Freeze-drying mushrooms can be done in a way that not only makes the mushroom convenient to eat, but largely maintains its chemical integrity.

There are many pieces of anecdotal evidence on the benefits of freeze-dried mushrooms. A published paper by Ikekawa et al (1969) on the use of freeze-dried water extract of shiitake is but one of hundreds of examples of freeze-dried fungi being used in medicinal research.

This point is important because a recent reference material on ABM claims that freeze-drying destroys ABM's active components. There was no scientific evidence sighted to support this claim and it is simply not true.

Acknowledgements

I must thank my parents for many, many things but especially the golden opportunity to spend summers in a place where there was a lake, a forest, friends and very few cars. You and Dave are my main audience- I wrote this with you in mind.

Motone Hayakawa opened my eyes to ABM and I will forever be thankful for her patience, intelligence, understanding and beautiful lunches. The time she spent instructing me as we set up the homepage is a time I will always treasure. Her introduction to the Taiai Company and to Dr. Iwasaki (whom I would also like to thank) was invaluable.

Anyone who knows the Nakameguro area of Tokyo knows that it is full of some of Japan's most talented and creative people. I was unbelievably lucky to be able to use the creative facilities at stile and at Vanryuji Studio. At stile I shared office space with Tamala, a computer-generated movie star. At Vanryuji I looked out upon a Japanese temple complete with a pond and a beautiful garden. In the same part of town I received encouragement from Akiyoshi Kumiko. Finally, another Nakameguro resident, Mamoru Ofuku, provided me with his guidance in matters literary, practical and spiritual. Peggi and Paul from www.popwars.com and Arnaud Rastoul from Gam Audy Japon also helped make this book a reality. Thanks also to Gary Shaw.

Sachiko Yoshita- your patience and support carried me through the dark moments. Thank you.

While visiting Tokyo from Hungary, Dr. Gabor Somlyai kindly allowed me to question him about the immune system and cell division. Dr. Somlyai's pioneering work on the role of deuterium in the cell cycle and the development of deuterium-depleted water as a cancer treatment is revolutionary and inspiring. Also my sincere thanks to the Interquest Corporation and Jaszai-san for arranging the time with Dr. Somlyai.

Two doctors from the Medical College of Ohio, Dr. Hermann Schut and Dr. Paul F. Lehmann also generously shared their time and resources with me. I am still telling people about the way we met!

In New York Lucie McAllister, George Lefteris, Arleen Schloss, Stuart Pyle, Dub Rogers and Steve Pagnotta have always provided inspirational support and this project was no exception. Also in New York, NewLife magazine was very helpful and I thank them for their cover page story on ABM. The New Life Expo a few weeks after September 11, 2001 is one I will never forget and the beautiful people at Northern Edge Flax-James, Leslie and DeAnne, made that time as positive as it could be under the circumstances.

The New York Public Library and the New York Botanical Gardens provided the opportunity to eliminate some of the mystery surrounding W.A. Murrill, the man who named agaricus blazei.

ABM enabled me to make two new friends in Baltimore-Bob Greene and Mary Bernard.

I also wish to mention the Bioneers (www.bioneers.com). The October 2001 session and the chance to hear Dr. Andrew Weill, Dr. Tieraona Low Dog, Dr. Larry Dorsey and many other people was an once-in-a-lifetime event. The mycological presentations by Paul Stamets were the equivalent of watching Picasso paint, Michael Jordan dunk or Orson Welles drink wine. I left his sessions full of hope.

I would like to thank many of my long-time friends in Toledo, Ohio- especially Larry Lough, Ed Schweickart and Pat Desmond.

In Singapore I would like to thank my designer, Emeline (www.realartificial.com) for her patience, Koh for the nice portrait and especially and everyone at 148 Emerald Hill Rd for their support.

Lastly, to Mrs. Dudek and her family, thank you for your trust in me.

To all of the people mentioned above and countless others all over the world, I sincerely thank you.

Stephen Black
Tokyo, August 10, 2002
Revised in Singapore, December 17, 2002

Note: In this book, "Agaricus blazei *Murill,* ABM, and agaricus are used interchangeably. The author's preference when discussing the mushroom is "ABM". In Japan and among some professionals in the American mushroom world, the word "Himematsutake" is also used. Himematsutake translates as "princess mushroom".

Agaricus Blazei Murill

Domain: Eukarya
Kingdom: Fungi
Phylum: Asidiomycota
Class: Hymenomcetes
Order: Agaricales
Family: Agaricaceae
Genus: Agaricus
Species: Agaricus blazei *Murill*

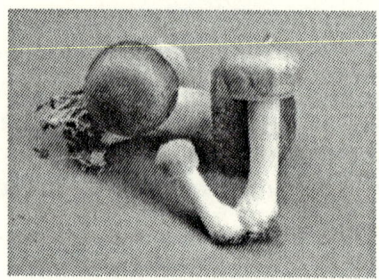

Named by an American naturalist who discovered the mushroom on a lawn in Florida, it has been called "The Mushroom of God" by generations of Brazilians and is the best-selling health supplement in Japan.
Researched and used for its effects against cancer, arthritis, asthma, allergies, and several other immune-system related diseases, Agaricus blazei *Murill* shows promise for many other modern diseases, including AIDS/HIV.

History, Facts and Goals

"If one is a beginner, he is like an explorer in a new country with an abundance of attractive fruit nearby which may be good or may be rank poison: he cannot tell without trying it, unless some native, who has learned from his own and others experiences, shares his knowledge with him."

- **William Alphonso Murill, mycologist, world- traveler and assistant director of the New York Botanical Gardens. The Agaricus blazei *Murill* mushroom bears his name.**

Like most Americans, I am concerned about staying healthy. Unlike most Americans, however, I have spent a considerable amount of time in Japan. It was in Tokyo during the winter of 2000 I first heard of Agaricus blazei *Murill* and its incredible characteristics. To make a long story short, I have written this book primarily to increase awareness of ABM, especially among those people concerned about cancer, AIDS/HIV, arthritis, allergies and other immune system related diseases.

Toni (Motone) Hayakawa, a mother, a neighbor and a registered pharmacist asked me to help convert her Japanese-language homepage into English. As we worked together, my initial skepticism became transformed into belief and ultimately a life-changing passion. (I have done my best to temper my passion with an open mind regarding all studies and research. I am not a blind fanatic believing in the power of ABM. I have looked everywhere for any negative side effects of ABM and have found none. Some, but certainly not all Japanese research papers are poor and would not be accepted outside of Japan. There are also many questionable cases of anecdotal evidence. I have avoided using anything that may fall into either of these two categories).

I believe that sharing knowledge about ABM is vitally important because ABM has an established history of research and has been used to improve the health of countless people. I have experienced the healing power of ABM in myself and in those close to me. Most likely due to the use of ABM, I have seen tumors become "nonexistent" in people close to me.

ABM is being used in Japan, Brazil and China as a food, as a health supplement, as a prophylactic, a stimulant to the immune system and as an adjuvant in cancer therapy. Most of the information on ABM is in Japanese, Portuguese or Chinese.

Since its introduction to Japan in the 1970's, the use of ABM has grown continuously. There are now at least 250 companies selling about 500 million dollars worth of ABM a year. (The 2000 edition of the Japanese Health Industry newsletter used a figure which was the equivalent of 300 million U.S. dollars. In his book, <u>Growing Gourmet and Medicinal Mushrooms</u>, the American mushroom authority Paul Stamets used the figure of 600 million U.S. dollars). The products include dried ABM, powdered ABM, freeze-dried ABM and liquid extracts. I believe access to information about ABM's historical and contemporary use as a health supplement should be available to all.

I have found NO significant negative side effects in my research. I have reviewed dozens of scientific papers and I have heard literally hundreds of stories about individuals who have recovered their health by using ABM.

Allow me to stop and digress a moment. I have just mentioned "stories about people who have used ABM to recover their health". The following are <u>personal</u> anecdotes:

- My partner, Hayakawa-san, for example, helped a neighbor recover from cancer of the esophagus by using freeze-dried ABM exclusively. - One of my neighbors in Ohio is in very good condition after going through mild radiation therapy over a year ago and using ABM as well as a Amazonian herb called "cat's claw". Her doctors were surprised that she had no scarring resulting from her radiation therapy. She is in her early 70s. She once had a tumor the size of a ping-pong ball on her portal vein. According to her family doctor, the tumor is now "nearly non-existent". Additionally, a tumor in her eye has disappeared with no treatment other than ABM, cat's claw and prayer. I can provide lab tests/doctor's testimony upon request.

- As part of a video documentary I am making, I interviewed a woman in her 80s who had stage 4 (the most serious) liver cancer over ten years ago. I also interviewed her son who described how the doctors had given up hope due to the size of the three tumors in her liver. Her recovery was due exclusively to the use of ABM liquid extract.

The above stories are called anecdotal evidence by doctors and researchers. Some see these stories as dangerous because they are unscientific-the tumors could have disappeared because of some other effect. Others may be more open-minded and may give the story some importance, especially if there are many such anecdotes.

I understand both sides. My position is to only speak about those cases which I have been involved in, as these cases are a part of my life; my experiences. For me to deny them is wrong and it is equally wrong for me to say that what happened in the cases I describe will happen to others. Based on my studies and experiences, I believe Agaricus blazei *Murill* can have positive effects upon health and believe it should be part of a healthy diet and lifestyle. The purpose of this book is to share the knowledge and experiences I have acquired while researching ABM so the reader may be able to make an informed judgement about the use of ABM in his or hers own life.

One last thought on this topic involves the concept of clinical trials. Clinical trials are tests involving humans-the final phase of testing before a drug becomes a medicine certified by the FDA.

Only in China have I been able to find cases of clinical testing presently happening. Obviously, however, ABM has been eaten for hundreds, if not thousands of years.

I have been asked," If ABM is so good and so popular in Japan, why don't doctors in the United States know about it?"

It is a very good question especially when we learn that, in 1917, the mushroom was discovered on a lawn in Florida and named by an American, W.A. Murrill.

Native Brazilians used ABM in their diets before and after this discovery, but, in the industrialized world, nothing seems to have happened until about fifty years later.

In 1965 two Americans, W.J. Sinden from the University of Pennsylvania and Dr. E.D. Lambert from Lambert Laboratories documented the fact that in an area of Brazil near Sao Paolo where people ate ABM frequently there were very few cancers or immune-system related diseases. Although research papers were presented shortly afterward presented at the University of Pennsylvania, no major developments in the United States' medical community were initiated.

The medical industry at the time was much more geared to creating pharmaceuticals and medical technologies and the idea a mushroom eaten by natives could be effective against cancer was ignored. Western medicine tends to break parts of plants down and patent them. Penicillin and aspirin are examples of this approach.

In Japan, however, things were different.
About the same time that the Sinden and Lambert were visiting Sao Paolo, a Japanese man who had been born and raised in the Piedade area outside of Sao Paolo returned to Japan. He introduced the mushroom to the Iwade Mushroom Institute in Mie Prefecture. The spores were cultured and grown. They were known by their Portuguese names, which when translated mean "The Mushroom of God" or "The Mushroom of the Sun".

"Princess mushroom" is the translation of "Himematsutake", the Japanese name created by the researchers. It wasn't until 1967 that a Belgian scientist, Dr. Heinemann, correctly identified them by their scientific name, Agaricus blazei *Murill*. The Iwade Mushroom Institute became influential in establishing ABM in Japan.

In 1970, Shoji Shibata, a professor from the Pharmacological department of Tokyo University and Dr. Ikegawa, a physician from the Japan National Cancer Center, jointly researched ABM. Together, they presented papers to the Japan Pharmacological Association, the Japan Cancer Association and elsewhere. Their research focused mainly on the anti-tumor properties of the beta-glucans found in ABM.

In 1980 papers were presented to the Japan Cancer Society showing that the beta glucan found in ABM is effective against Erlich's ascites carcinoma, sigmoid colonic cancer, ovarian cancer, breast cancer, lung cancer, liver cancer and solid cancer. The ABM industry in Japan can be said to have started at that time.

Initially, there was little advertising about ABM and word-of-mouth testimonials were a major means of publicity. The Japanese medicinal home delivery system eventually introduced the mushroom to thousands of households. The Japanese now buy an estimated 90% of all the ABM produced in the world. There are books, occasional TV documentaries, homepages, and many celebrity testimonials. One book, called *The Wonder Food Against Cancer*, is in its 63rd printing. In Japan, Coca-Cola launched an herbal tea in the spring of 2002 that contains ABM as well as Chinese herbs. ABM is finding its way into foods as well. Some of the Japanese ABM companies are trying to create a market for ABM in the U.S. and an American domestic ABM industry is in its infancy. A Hawaiian company is supplying Chinese hospitals and researchers with high grade ABM for research purposes.

In the U.S. the ABM market is ready to explode. A search on Yahoo for the words agaricus blazei murill in March of 2001 showed only one site. At the time of this writing, August 2002, nearly 500 sites were displayed. The American mushroom expert Paul Stamets rightly calls A*garicus* blazei *Murill* a rising star.

Since most of the research on ABM has been about its effects on the immune system and its effects against tumors, this book may appear to be focussed on the "Big C"-cancer. This is not the case- I am most enthusiastic about ABM as a preventative. However, as the Japanese expression says," No one wants to fix the roof when the sun is shining." It has been my experience so far that those who are most interested in ABM are those who already have cancer or know someone who does.

I am planning to update this notebook and the first revision will include the big "A"s -anthrax, AIDS, allergies and arthritis. I also plan to include more original interviews, illustrations and photos.
The purpose of this book and future revisions is to provide an up-to-date resource of information on all aspects and uses of the Agaricus blazei *Murill* mushroom.

The second goal of this book is to express an appreciation of simplicity, a renewed respect for nature and illustrate the reality that our internal health is a reflection of the external world. A sick planet means sick people. Let's make earth healthy...

Third goal: Agaricus blazei *Murill* being sold as a salad garnish in fast food restaurants by 2005 as a result of an increased public consciousness about ABM. *The ABM Notebook* aims to put Agaricus blazei *Murill* in the mainstream of popular culture.

This book is meant to provide the reader with a solid core of information so he or she may make informed decisions about the use of ABM as quickly as possible. As mentioned, a more thorough version for doctors and researchers is on its way, but this involves translations and copyright issues which will take time to resolve.

Please share the information in this book with your doctor when making decisions about your health.

ABM in the World of Mushrooms

To truly understand Agaricus blazei *Murill*, it is important to know the historical and contemporary use of mushrooms. Mushrooms have been eaten by humans for a very long time- the oldest image of a mushroom is found in a cave 5000 years old. Mushrooms have been used as food, medicine, fuel and a means of spiritual enlightenment continually throughout mankind's history.

The Chinese recognized the medicinal value of mushrooms very early. Traditional Chinese Medicine (TCM) refers to the reishi mushroom as "The Herb of Immortality" and it was used more than 2000 years ago. It was known for its beneficial effects on health and was associated with longevity, sexual power, wisdom and happiness. Reishi continues to be used extensively in China, Korea and Japan and, to a lesser extent, throughout the world.

Another very well known mushroom is Coriolus Versicolor, also known as turkey tail, yun zhi or kawaratake. From this mushroom a government (Japan) approved anticancer drug called "Krestin "or PSK has been created. Several hundred million dollars worth are sold annually. PSK has been shown to reduce cancers, stimulate interleukin production in human cells and is a scavenger of free-radical oxidizing compounds.

There are many other mushrooms which have been used and studied throughout Asian history, including maitake and shiitake.

ABM entered the world of Asian medicinal mushrooms very recently- the early 1970s. Not native to Asia, it was completely unknown but because the medical and research communities were familiar with the idea of using mushrooms medicinally, ABM was accepted. Undoubtedly its warm welcome was due to the small but impressive amount of research on its role as an immune system enhancer and anti-tumor effects. It is now being grown in China, Korea, the United States and elsewhere. It is now not only the best-selling mushroom product in Japan but there it is also is the best-selling health product.

Some of the many ads and fliers for Agaricus blazei *Murill*. In Japan, over 250 companies sell about $500 million dollars worth of ABM annually. In the spring of 2002, Coca Cola introduced a tea to the Japanese market which included Agaricus.
(Photo/digital composition copyright 2002 Larry Lough)

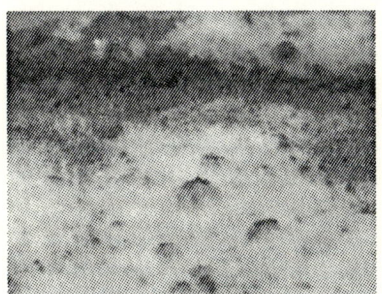 Agaricus blazei *Murill* mycellia

 Once the mycellial mass senses the proper atmospheric and nutritional requirements are present, fruiting bodies appear....

 which, about one week later, become...

 the mushrooms known as

 Agaricus blazei *Murill*

ABM IN THE WILD

An awareness of the conditions that ABM experiences in the wild may help to explain why it has evolved the way it has and why the results of that evolution benefit both the mushroom itself and the human body.

Agaricus blazei *Murill* is a fungus. Fungi get nourishment by breaking down the materials in which they are growing. They are Earth's recyclers.

When we see a mushroom, we are actually seeing the "fruit" of what is called the mycelium. Mycelium are networks of thread-like cells. Once these cells have reached a certain state of maturity and have favorable internal and environmental conditions- (meaning that they are well fed and the humidity, sunlight etc. are suitable), they form the beginnings of the mushroom. The mushroom grows and forms spores, which are released to begin the cycle once more.

Why does this pattern result in beneficial components?

The environment in which the mushroom lives provides us with clues. ABM in the wild likes wooded areas. It feeds upon dead organic matter and prefers areas full of rotting plants. These areas are full of bacteria, germs, life-threatening chemicals and other fungal competitors.

Animals eat food and then digest it. Fungi do the reverse, creating digestable food and then eating it. Fungi "eat" by secreting enzymes and acids, breaking up the large chemical molecules found in plant matter into simpler compounds. ABM is a secondary decomposer, meaning it can only eat if a primary decomposer lived in the area previously. After eating, a primary decomposer leaves behind partially broken down food, which attracts other fungi, bacteria, yeasts, etc. To survive in this environment, ABM has developed chemical defenses so that it may eat without becoming infected.

When ABM "eats" it is actually secreting digestive chemicals into the environment around it. It then absorbs these secretions and the nutrients they have made available. This process of disinfecting and digesting the nutrients in a hostile environment undoubtedly resulted in a life form with a strong ability to chemically defend itself.

The most famous region for producing ABM is the area near Sao Paolo, Brazil, although it is also found in the hot and humid areas north and south of the equator in the Americas.

The Sao Paolo region is known for its unusual weather. It can get as hot as 35° Celsius (95° during the day and as low as 20-25°Celsius° (68-77° Fahrenheit)at night. There are daily rainstorms and the humidity is usually 80%. These growing conditions are thought to be ideal and explain why domestically cultivating ABM was such a challenge initially.

ABM as a Food

The Chinese say "The roots of food and medicine are the same" and ABM exemplifies this beautifully. It is not only full of recognized anti-tumor components; it is delicious. It is a member of the agaricus family of mushrooms, which were being eaten by the people of Agaria in Eastern Europe two thousand years ago. The mushroom that the Agarians ate had the classic mushroom shape with a stem and a cap.

Beneath the cap, gills radiate from the center.

It was in the Netherlands in 1527 that the usage of "agaricus" as a name for a family of mushrooms with these characteristics began. There are dozens of agaricus family members, which is why the full name of Agaricus Blazei Murill is used. (This is not the case in Japan where ABM is referred to as "a ga ree ku su").

Another member of the agaricus family is a mushroom called agaricus brunnescens, one of the most widely cultivated mushrooms in the United States. It is the button mushroom that is found in most salad bars and grocery stores. It does not contain as many of the components found in ABM.

Another member of the agaricus family often found on the dining table is the Portobello mushroom, the centerpiece of a multibillion global industry.

Dr. Andrew Weil, on his highly recommended website (www.drweil.com) answers a reader's question about the mushroom's effects on breast cancer. He described ABM as "tasty". Dr. Weil's website is an excellent reference for integrative medicine, although at the time of this writing he has written little about ABM. He posts excellent information about other medicinal mushrooms like shiitake, reishi and maitake and soon I look forward to reading more of his thoughts about ABM.

In his excellent reference book, *Growing Gourmet and Medicinal Mushrooms*, Paul Stamets says ABM "imparts a sweet almond flavor, delicate but distinct, a symphony of flavors that linger long after consumption". His description of the beautiful color changes during cooking -"the slices of mushrooms undergo a mesmerizing color change from white to strong golden yellow"- gives another reason to look forward to the day when fresh ABM is available from the local grocer.

In Ehime, Japan, close to a company that grows ABM, there is restaurant using ABM in a variety of traditional dishes. There one can order ABM grilled, in soups, stews-even sushi.

Although statistics are hard to come by, the most common form of ABM is probably the dried form. It is not recommended to be eaten by itself, but should be made into a tea or used in soups and sauces. It is important to eat the body of the dried mushroom after cooking.

There is also a freeze-dried form. This form can be eaten directly from the bag or used in cooking. Those who are fond of mushrooms usually like the taste. This author finds it very pleasant, especially with a drop or two of good olive oil and a pinch of sea salt. Add a cracker, tiny trip of Parmesan or Swiss cheese and a slice of tomato and you have a very healthy gourmet fast food.

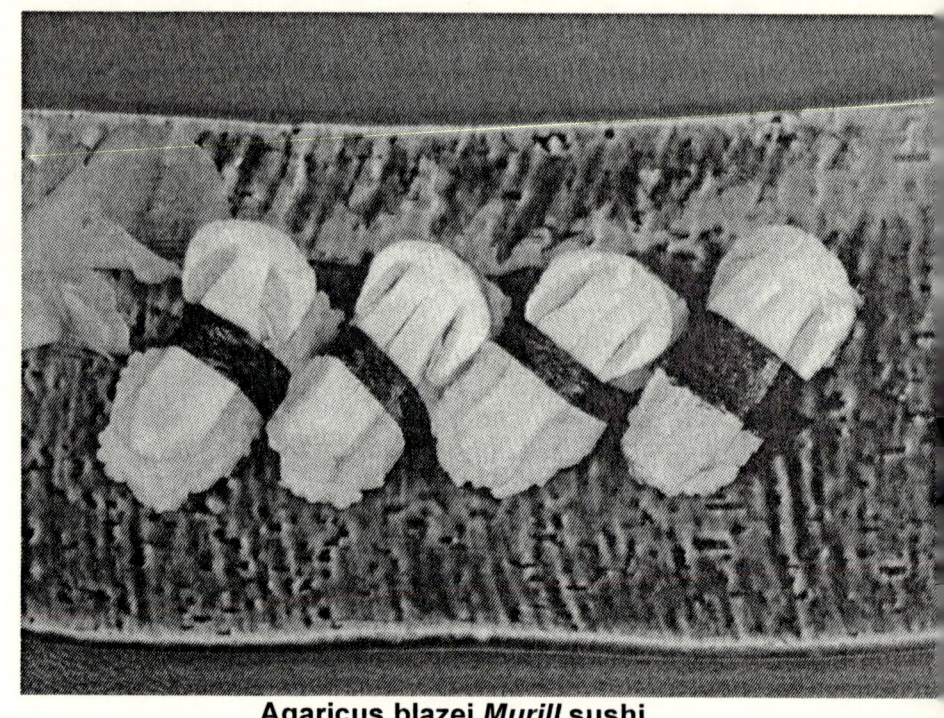
Agaricus blazei *Murill* sushi

the Takasukas

the Hamaichi restaurant

I have photographed sushi in Japan, the cuisine of Louisiana, and French chefs. Bill O'Reilly(from Fox TV) mentioned my mom's lasagna on national tv. I once shared a table at Manhattan's Oyster Bar with a former food editor of the New York Times.

Agaricus and beef sautéed with grated Japanese radish sauce(agaricus to niku no oroshi sauce itame)

Agaricus and seafood with balsamic vinegar dressing (agricus to gyokaibui no balsamic vinegar)

Shinsen® Agaricus salad

Agaricus tempura

Agaricus soup (yakuzen dobinmushi)

I definitely appreciate food and I looked forward to this meal like no other.

We picked ABM at 11:30 a.m. and ninety minutes later, one of the most unforgettable meals of my life began with delicately dry sake.

WHAT DOES ABM DO IN THE BODY?

When eaten as a cooked mushroom, ABM first does what all foods do to the body- it stimulates the mouth, tongue and nose. Even before it is eaten, the delicate almondy scent of the mushroom sends the body flavorful messages. In the mouth, the taste buds report their pleasant and various findings to the brain as the teeth crush the crunchy stem and the slippery cap. Digestive processes have begun. ABM is easily digested and immediately the mushroom bits are dismantled by digestive juices.

When ABM enters the body as a tea, extract or pill, the mouth is just a way to get the ABM into the stomach. As a rule, these forms enter the bloodstream more rapidly than the solid forms, the liquid extract form being the fastest. They are also eliminated more quickly. Two important components of ABM are not easily digested, however.

The first is dietary fiber. Doctors and advertisements continually tell us to add fiber to our diet– and for good reason. Fiber absorbs cholesterol, toxins and cancerous or cancer-causing materials in our body and carries them out of the body.

The second non-digestible component of ABM is a collection of sugar molecules called beta glucans. Books have been written about beta glucan and companies are trying to synthesize it. It has been compared to penicillin, another medicine derived from fungus.

"Glucan was found to be an effective drug in inducing macrophage-mediated destruction in malignant lesions in animals and humans." Dr. P. Mansel M.D., a doctor at the McGill University Cancer Research Center in Montreal has been quoted as saying. There are many more quotes and many tests conducted by internationally recognized physicians and institutes. The bibliography at the back of this book may be of interest to those physicians and researchers seeking more specific information. I also suggest looking at the United States Government's own National Library of Medicine web site, PubMed. (www.ncbi.nlm.nih.gov)

The importance of beta glucan cannot be overstated. However, one should keep in mind the fact that there is no "magic bullet" against cancer. To quote Dr. Andrew Weil, "Nature never uses just one molecule,"

According to studies at Ehime University in Japan, beta glucan extract has less effect than the whole mushroom. Studies there are currently focusing on other compounds in ABM that explain its effectiveness. Just as eating fresh whole fruits are the best way to get vitamin C, so it may be with beta glucan and ABM.

In mentioning vitamin C I am reminded of some undocumented reports claiming that vitamin C (and ginger as well) helps the body break up beta glucans into more easily utilized pieces. The suggested amount was 1000 grams. A slice of ginger and a glass of orange juice when taking ABM would be delicious and healthy additions to anyone's diet.

Of all mushrooms tested, Agaricus blazei *Murill* has one of the highest concentrations of beta glucan.

ABM is full of protein. The mushroom expert Paul Stamets has found this to be "one of the most protein-rich of all cultivated mushrooms". He also found carbohydrates and fat among many other beneficial ingredients.

Agaricus contains melanin, for example, a protein used by the body to produce hair. Bones and teeth benefit from the Vitamin B1 and B2 found in ABM. Dietary fibers as well as the unsaturated fatty acids like linolin found in ABM have been found to reduce blood pressure, reduce cholesterol levels and the risk of arteriosclerosis.

ABM also contains steroids that directly affect carcinoma cells and inhibit cancer growth. Steroids derived specifically from ABM have been shown to inhibit cancer growth in test tubes. Steroids from other sources have been recognized for their anticancer effects, especially the prevention of uterine cancer. These steroids are not to be confused with the performance enhancing steroids taken by athletes.

Researchers at the University of Tokyo found that ABM contains an essential fatty acid called linoleic acid. This acid is known for its antimutagenic properties. They also found an antibacterial agent in

ABM.

Like any other food, ABM is broken down and used by every part of the body. Its relationship to the immune system and its anti-cancer effects are well known, but all parts of the body benefit directly or indirectly from ABM.

This is why the preventive use of ABM is so important. Instead of repairing itself and carrying around life-draining illnesses, the body has the energy for maintenance and repair-what we can refer to as anti-aging. When we start to prevent illnesses and give the body the nourishment it was designed for, we look and feel better.

Who may benefit from ABM?

Although everyone may enjoy the taste of ABM as a delicious food and as a daily health supplement, ABM may also be considered as a treatment for
- Men, women and children with impaired or suppressed immune systems
- Men women and children with a high occurrence of infectious diseases, including colds and flu
- Those people with poor nutritional habits
- Those people with allergies or skin inflammations
- Cancer patients who are undergoing chemotherapy and/or radiotherapy
- Individuals over the age of 40 experiencing a slowdown in immune system function
- Those individuals expose to UV radiation, electromagnetic fields and/or toxic chemicals
- Pilots, passengers and airline staff who make frequent high altitude flights
- Individuals with chronic diseases such as diabetes, chronic inflammation and chronic fatigue
- Men or women at high risk for arteriosclerosis
- Professional and amateur athletes or anyone who works out intensively
- Persons under physical or emotional stress

Health benefit	ABM Component
Effect of absorbing and discharging cancerous materials	Non-digestive Beta D glucan Hetero polysaccharide Chitin
Reducing blood pressure	Beta glucans Polysaccharide protein compounds, RNA, compounds
Hypotensive effect; reducing cholesterol, reducing arteriosclerosis	Dietary fiber and unsaturated fatty acid such as linolic acid composing lipid

Source: The Chemical Times, ISSN 0285-2446
Kanto Chemical Co. Inc. 1989, NO.1 131 Volumes in all) extract from page 12-21 Takashi Mizuno: Pharmacological Effects of Fungi and its Applications

WHAT IS BETA GLUCAN?

Beta glucan is the name given to a family of sugar molecules (also called polysaccharides). They were first discovered about thirty years ago and have been studied by many institutions including Tulane, Harvard and several Japanese universities. Beta glucans could be as important to immunology as penicillin was to the world of antibiotics.

Of all mushrooms tested to this day, ABM has more beta glucan than most others. Actually, it has several types of beta glucan. The two which have been studied the most are beta glucan -3 and beta glucan 1-6. The numbers refer to the way chemists describe the molecular structure.

In the molecular world, beta glucan molecules are considered to be very large and this has raised questions about how easily they can be digested. It has been reported on the Internet that vitamin C breaks down the molecule so it is more easily digested. There was no study sighted to support this.

Beta glucan is known for the following properties:
- **Correcting and strengthening the immune system**
- **Successfully treating allergies and skin conditions**
- **Used as an adjuvant before and after chemotherapy and radiotherapy**
- **An anti-oxidant and assists free radical scavengers**
- **Used by athletes for its healing and muscle tissue building effects**
- **Has beneficial effects on arteriosclerosis and reduces cholesterol**
- **Offers protection from radiation**

The most impressive study regarding beta glucan was performed by the United States' Armed Forces Radiobiological Institute. Mice were given lethal doses of radiation and then given beta glucan. The result was that 70% of those mice survived with no ill effects. The Institute carried out research in other areas as well. According to M.L. Patchen, Ph.D. from the Institute's Department of Experimental Hematology and Radiation Sciences, "**Glucan (Beta-1, 3-D) has been shown to enhance macrophage production dramatically and to increase nonspecific host resistance to a variety of bacterial, fungal and parasitic infections.**"

In other words, beta glucan increased the number of macrophages-those cells which eat unwanted cells and debris-including tumors. Also the amount of cytotoxic granules-the macrophages' chemical weapons against cancer and invaders-was increased.

Dr. Patchen's remarks about nonspecific host resistance mean that the part of the immune system which is capable of eliminating unwanted organisms and materials from the body without any "teaching" is increased, the result being that sicknesses caused by bacteria, fungi and parasites can be minimized.

In 1995, another study, by Dr. Mamdooh Ghneum Ph.D. from King Drew Medical Center of UCLA, also found that ABM not only increased the number of NK cells, but also made each individual cell more powerful. He presented his findings to the Ninth World Immunology Congress held in San Francisco:

"**In the present study, we evaluate the ability of Agaricus to stimulate in vivo Natural Killer cell activity in mice. The results demonstrated that the induction of NK activity was very significant (38-49 fold increase over control).**"

There are many types of beta glucans and one form is derived from yeast cells. This form is classified by the FDA as "Generally Regarded as Safe". No negative side effects have been recorded. Although yeast cells and other mushrooms contain beta glucans, the beta glucan molecules in ABM are unique in their chemical properties.

Cancer treatments based on beta glucan derived from other mushrooms are already on the market and it is reasonable to think that eventually ABM will "catch up" and its unique beta glucans will be the basis of an anti-cancer treatment.

In the June 1996 issue of The Townsend Letter, an article appeared by Dr. D.J. Carrow. The article was called "Beta1-3 Glucan as a Primary Immune Activator."

"Over the past 11 months I have been able to convince five out of eight breast cancer patients who were undergoing radiation therapy to consume one capsule of beta 1.3/1.6 glucan (NSC-24-3mg) three times per day. To date, I have observed that none of the patients using NSC-24 have suffered from any type of radiation injury to the skin, while the three patients who chose not to use NSC-24 all show signs of extensive radiation damage to the skin."

Polysaccharides discovered in Agaricus blazei *Murrill*	
AB-P	Agaricus Blazei Polysaccharide(Beta glucan 1.6)
Beta glucan 1.3	
ATOM	Antitumor Organic Substance Mie
AB-FP	Agaricus Blazei culture filtrate polysaccharide
b-glycan F1-o-a-b	
a-glycan FA1	
b-galactoglycan FA-1-a-b	
Nucleic acid(RNA) FA-2-b-b	
Proteinic glycan FIII 2-b	
Xyloglucan FIV-2-b	

The Immune System

The immune system has been described as that part of the body that distinguishes between what is self and what is nonself.

The immune system includes the lymph system, the blood system, bone marrow and more. There is evidence supporting the idea that emotions and stress can influence the immune system, so in this sense, even the brain can be considered part of the immune system.

The skin is a simple example of the immune system as it clearly defines what is in the body and what is not. It does a great job, but it has limitations. For example, how would the skin know that there are bacteria on the sandwich we had for lunch?

Things or organisms like viruses, bacteria, parasites, foreign objects and certain chemicals are all non-self and the body reacts to them differently. This reaction is intelligent and organized. It utilizes strategy, analysis, experience and a number of forceful weapons, mechanisms and executioners. In short, the immune system wages plans and executes warlike strategies on anything that it believes is non-self.

A piece of glass, for example, is practically inert- its presence does not immediately cause the immune system to attack it, although the immune system will do its best to repair any damage the glass's entry into the body may have caused.

A bacterium, however, gives off chemical signals which tell the body that the bacterium is not self. Different parts of the immune system detect the intruder and relay the information to the headquarters of the immune system. The immune system devises a strategy, sends out the appropriate weapons with the appropriate troops and attacks. It records the battle plan so the next battle will be more organized, more efficient.

This is the basis of immunity and explains how vaccinations work when a child receives a weakened bit of smallpox the immune system breaks it down, analyses it and records all of the important data. The next time that smallpox enters the body, the body pulls up the smallpox records and uses the same strategy it used previously with the result that the smallpox virus cannot establish itself in the body.

Besides annihilating what needs to be annihilated, the immune system gets rid of pathogens, toxic chemicals, and tumor cells. It helps the body repair and heals itself. Finally, the immune system maintains balance, or homeostasis, in the body.

An organ transplant is a serious matter for the immune system. Whether an organ is "accepted "or "rejected", depends on what the immune system thinks of the transplanted organ. If it is perceived as not self, the immune system ends out its troops and begins to attack.

This same concept happens in what are called autoimmune diseases. In autoimmune diseases the immune system loses the ability to tell the difference between self and non-self. It starts to send troops to destroy itself. The body destroys its own cells, cell components or organs. This is what happens in diseases like allergies, asthma, rheumatoid arthritis, dermatitis, diabetes, lupus, multiple sclerosis and fibromyalgia.

ABM helps the immune system maintain homeostasis, a sense of balance. This condition of being balanced makes it less likely the immune system will attack itself and more likely that diseases and invaders which damage health will be eliminated.

Medical Department of Tokyo University, The National Cancer Center Laboratory and Tokyo College of Pharmacy Anti-Cancer Results

Name Of Fungus	Daily Dosage mmg.	Rate Of Complete Recovery	Anti-cancer effect
Agaricus blazei *Murill*	10	90.0%	99.4%
Grifola umbellate (Zhu Ling or Chinese Scerotium)	10	90.0%	98.5%
Phellinus yucatensis	30	87.5%	96.5%
Phellinus igniaius	30	66.7%	87.4%
Lenzites betulina	30	57.1%	70.2%
Tricholoma matsutake (Matsutake)	30	55.5%	91.3%
Lentinus edodes(Shiitake)	30	54.5%	80.7%
Coriolus versicolor (Turkey tail, Kawaratake or Cloud Mushroom)	30	50.0%	77.5%
Pleurotus osteatus (Tree Oyster Mushroom)	30	45.5%	75.3%
Elfringia applanata	30	45.5%	64.9%
Fomitopsis pincicola	30	33.3%	61.2%
Fomitopsis cytisna	30	30.3%	44.2%
Pholiota nameko (Nameko)	30	30.0%	86.5%
Flammulina velutipes (Enoki)	30	30.0%	81.1%
Ganoderma Lucidum (Reishi)	30	20.0%	77.8%

The chart compares the effects of various mushrooms on tumors. To understand the chart fully, it is necessary to know scientists have developed a test in which guinea pigs get cancer. A cell called Sarcoma 180 is injected into animals which normally causes them to die within four to five weeks. The chart shows that ABM was the most effective against cancer among those mushrooms tested.

The anti-cancer effect rate indicates the percentage of guinea pigs that recovered fully from the cancer caused by the first injection of the sarcoma 180 vaccinations and in whom a second injection failed because the cells were unable to establish themselves. The test also revealed the fact ABM activates the immune system of normal tissue. When a virus or other external pathogens- such as cancer-enter the tissue, they are eaten or are chemically eliminated as a result of macrophage and interferon production. ABM caused an increased state of efficiency that prevented the multiplication, metastasis and re-occurrence of cancer cells. Another finding from the study found that metabolism was activated by revitalized normal biological tissue.

Finally it should be noted that the amount of ABM extract used was almost a third less than the majority of the other fungi tested. This high rate of effectiveness is probably due to the uniqueness of its beta glucan content.

THE BODY, ABM AND CANCER

The human body has very specific defenses against cancer, viruses, bacteria and other invaders. There are cells in our body which can attack cancer and the chemicals which we create naturally are better than any pharmaceutical company can make. The chart below shows how ABM affects those natural defenses.

Defense	Activity	Interaction with ABM
Macrophages	Eat invaders (viruses, cancer)	Macrophages increase dramatically in number after ABM has been eaten
Natural Killer Cells	Kill cells infected by viruses as well cancer cells	ABM stimulates the production of NK cells, which kill unhealthy cells
Lymphokines	Many activities, including the destruction of uhealthy cells and stimulating macrophages	ABM appears to increase the efficiency of lymphokines,
Interleukins	Enable communication to happen between cells	ABM appears to increase the efficiency of interleukins
Apoptosis	Cellular suicide in which old and diseased cells destroy themselves	ABM increases apoptosis
Tumor Necrosis Factor	The body's own chemotherapy which kills tumor cells	ABM appears to increase the efficiency of TNF

CANCER

Because cancer is one of the defining diseases of our times and because most of the ABM research has centered on cancer, a review of the disease is in order.

Cancers in humans rarely result from viruses or massive chemical input, although constantly increasing environmental chemical pollution is undoubtedly a factor in the majority of cancers. Our air, our food, our living environment- all probably contain chemicals which can disrupt the normal patterns of our cells.

The television reporter Bill Moyers had his blood analyzed as part of a program about health. His blood contained 84 pollutants, only one of which (lead), was in existence 60 years ago. The interaction of these pollutants within the body is unpredictable.

Genetics, stress and age are other factors in the cancer equation. Usually cancer occurs spontaneously because of a series of genetic disruptions. There are many types of cancer because there are many kinds of cells. Any type of cell can experience a genetic disruption. Blood cell, brain cell, lung or liver- cancer can occur anywhere. Depending on the type of cell, its physical location, the health and eating habits of the host etc, the cancer will be as unique as the body in which it is living.

A tumor one centimeter long probably started its life 4-5 years before it was detected. A tumor of this size is made up of about ten million cells. Because the host body is unaware of the tiny tumor, and because little pieces of the tumor are continually breaking off, it is very likely that at least one of those small pieces has already established a new colony of cancer somewhere else in the body. This process is called metastasis.

To reach that size, the cancer cells have done the following: they have ignored the usual self-regulation controls and have multiplied uncontrollably; they have manipulated or overridden those mechanisms which normally stop abnormal multiplication. It has also reactivated genes used in fetal development to metastasize. If it continues to grow, it will do its best to secure a nearby blood vessel. With nutrients secured, the tumor will grow more easily.

The immune system does not always perceive the tumor as something to be destroyed. Some cancer cells have the ability to chemically camouflage themselves as normal cells, for example.

Also, some tumors produce antigens, but they are not strong enough to make the immune system respond.

If metastasis does occur, it is good for cancer, bad for the body. That one tiny tumor and its' ten million cells shed tiny pieces of themselves continuously. These pieces can travel through the blood stream and the lymph system to anywhere else in the body. This characteristic is why doctors watch the five years following the initial treatment very carefully.

TEA

Before it was possible to extract, encapsulate or freeze-dry ABM, it was eaten as a cooked food or used in teas. In all cases heat is necessary to make the ingredients accessible to the body.

The standard amount of dried agaricus to be used as a preventative tea is half of a gram per cup of water. It can be flavored as desired with lemon, mint etc. It has been suggested that vitamin C should be taken in conjunction with the tea as the Vitamin C aids in making the polysaccharides available to the body.

Lastly, it is important to eat the body of the mushrooms used for the tea. It has been suggested that actually only a small portion of ingredients are released in the tea-making process and most remain in the body of the mushroom.

Frequently Asked Questions

Why should I take ABM?
ABM is a nutritious health supplement that is full of vitamins, minerals, amino acids, fiber and more. Additionally, it is full of beta glucan which has been studied for its anti-tumor activities. So far, no other food has been shown to contain as much beta glucan as ABM.
"The broad spectrum of immunopharmacological activities of beta glucan includes not only the modification of certain bacterial, fungal, viral and parasitic infection, but also inhibition of tumor growth."
Nicholas DiLuzio, Ph.D., department of Physiology, Tulane University School of Medicine.

Besides cancer, what other diseases have been studied in relation to ABM?
ABM has been used in research tests for cancer, radiation-related illnesses, high blood pressure and arteriosclerosis. However, there are many pieces of anecdotal evidence and testimonies about ABM being used successfully as a treatment for hepatitis C, atopic dermatitis, rheumatism, asthma and allergies.

How and why did you become involved with ABM?
Motone Hayakawa introduced me to ABM. She has a Japanese homepage devoted to the freeze-dried form. Because she was moving to the United States, she wanted to create an English version and asked me to help with the grammar, explanations, etc. The more she told me and the more I read, the more convinced I became that ABM was legitimate. The simple fact that over 250 companies sell about 500 million dollars worth of ABM speaks for itself.
It is also important to note that Hayakawa-san is a registered pharmacist and researched ABM for about two years before establishing a relationship with Taiai (our suppliers). She presented me with dozens of papers and books. Finally, her confidence and her success stories with the freeze-dried form convinced me that

this was not only worthy of my time, but also something that would benefit others. It was shocking to find out how little was known about ABM in the U.S. I became excited about educating others about something that is a household word in Japan.
I have always preferred simplicity in all areas related to health and nutrition. Eating a small piece of ABM daily is a natural extension of that idea.
Since May of 2001 I have eaten about one half gram of the freeze-dried form of ABM every day, more if I am traveling, under stress or in contact with sick people. Except for a one-day bout with food poisoning, I have been in good health.
I also eat flax and wheat germ daily and drink a tea made of Amazonian herbs. I eat as many fruits and vegetables as I can.

What is a typical day like for you in the world of ABM?
Actually, at this point I spend about an hour a day in the world of ABM. In the beginning, there was a lot of studying to do and the website took time to set up. Now however, I occasionally scan the net for ABM news, answer emails and try to write a little every day.
That is not to say my "ABM life" is boring.
The worst "excitement" is the kind in which someone is very sick and wants to try ABM as a last resort. The chemo isn't working, the radiation isn't working and the surgery didn't get it all. These emails and phone calls can become emotional.
We have not and never will say ABM is a cure for anything. In the laboratory, anti-tumor activity has been documented in rats and other animals. There have been hundreds, maybe thousands, of human success stories.
However, I fully understand the skepticism of people. My life before ABM was very full and I would not have made time for it unless I really thought it was special. Nothing, however, can be said to cure cancer in all of the people all of the time. It is personally disturbing, is to see friends, colleagues and relatives blindly accept the opinion of one doctor without considering the dozens of treatments available.
These minuses are offset by the good news of recoveries. Whether

an old friend or an unseen email correspondent, the joy is indescribable.
Most of the time though, my partner and I are doing mundane things like writing letters or trying to think of ways to increase sales. Also, we often get serious inquiries from individuals or companies. We spend a lot of time answering and researching questions-and then they buy it cheaper from someone else! With our counter we are able to see that our website hits come from all over the world. Military institutions, universities and hospitals have all visited us.
In May of 2001 I attended the NewLife Expo in Baltimore. In some ways it was a comedy of errors. I brought too much, no one knew what it was, it was expensive, the attendance was low, on and on. There was a baseball game happening at the same time and the only hotel available was the most expensive! However, a few people seemed to sense that ABM was something remarkable. Those "ABM pioneers" will always remain dear to me.
The second NewLife show I did was in New York in the middle of October 2001. Ground zero was still smoking and then, just a couple of days before the show's opening, the anthrax made the headlines. Envelopes containing anthrax had been received just a few blocks away from where the exhibition was to be held. The scare resulted in a strong gathering- mainly those who had a real belief in health, healing and wellness attended. Although it was a disaster financially, that time was full of energy, life and positive energy.
The first interested visitor was an elderly woman who probably would have been considered paranoid years ago. She was obviously thinking of ABM as a means of protecting herself against anthrax, although I was making no claims about any specific relation between the two.
I educated people about ABM and my favorite conversations were with those people interested in learning about ABM's preventive powers.
The first year, however, the sales were few and far between. I wrote a several articles that were published, but the Japanese level of ABM popularity remained very far off.

Although Motone-san and I hope to do shows again in the future, our focus right now is education; hence this book. We are doing our best to arrange clinical ABM testing and are also looking forward to ABM developments regarding AIDS/HIV.

Ultimately we hope to be in a position where we are providing very low cost ABM to all.(See the open letter to Bono and Bill Gates elsewhere in this book).

Is there a grading system for ABM?

I have seen a reference to a system in which Extra Gold is considered to have the most polysaccharides, followed by Gold and then Silver. This system, as far as I can tell, is not universally agreed upon nor followed. For researchers and growers, 4.8 grams of beta glucan per liter is an appropriate level. The average consumer may not find this information easily.

Another phrase I have seen is "clinical grade", but that was more of a sales pitch than an officially recognized standard.

To further complicate the issue, there are varieties such as Royal Agaricus, Oyama Agaricus Royal Sun Agaricus, Agaricus Neo-Blazei and more! Recently a new variety called Royal Agaricus was officially named by the British Botanical Association (official name: *Agaricus Sylvaticus* Shaeffer).

When considering where to buy ABM, the most important issue is trust. Like wine, there are many variables that go into making the final product. The more information offered to the consumer the better.

Does the company grow the ABM themselves? Do they buy it from a third party? If so, where? Is it organic or close to organic? Can the supplier answer your questions about heavy metal and pesticide content? Is the amount of ABM extract in a capsule clearly stated or is it a mixture?

The establishment of an internationally agreed upon ABM standards system will be a welcome step towards consistently high quality ABM products.

Where is ABM grown?
Although the cultivation of ABM began in Brazil, it is now grown in Japan, Hawaii, Indonesia, Korea and China. It is grown outdoors or indoors. It is possible to buy spores to grow your own ABM. Fungi Perfecti (www.fungiperfecti.com), a company specializing in mushroom products is a good source.

What is crucial to remember is that the growing of ABM is not that simple. Quality must be consistent from the time the growing medium is prepared to the final packaging. Pesticides, insecticides and chemicals to stimulate growth should be a major concern. In all cases, look for proof that the ABM has been grown organically.

Just like grapes, teas, and all grown produce, there can be huge differences in quality, taste and effectiveness. Quality is always more expensive. In Japan this fact has been used to take advantage of people.

Quality in ABM is defined as:
    a. Organically grown in organic soil,
    b. Grown harvested and packaged without contaminants such as molds or other fungi
    c. Constant monitoring for mutations, heavy metals and contaminants and
    d. Consistent beta glucan levels.

Can ABM be used with chemo?
Yes. ABM is considered an adjuvant, which means that it can be used alongside conventional treatments. No complications or side effects have been recorded.

Can pets benefit from ABM?
Yes. One gram daily for every 15 kilos is recommended as a prophylactic.

AN OPEN LETTER TO BONO, BILL GATES OR ANYONE WITH A LOT OF FAITH, HOPE AND TRUST

Hello.

I write to you today full of hope. I ask of you only that you find the time to read this brief letter with an open mind...

Growing Agaricus blazei *Murill* mushrooms is an efficient step towards changing the present situation in Africa. The initial costs are low, the maintenance is reasonable and the long-term benefits are revolutionary. I believe this for the following reasons.

1. **ABM is a food**. "*Agaricus Blazei Murill is one of the most protein rich of all cultivated mushrooms*" -Paul Stamets, internationally recognized mushroom authority and author of "Growing Gourmet and Medicinal Mushrooms".
2. **ABM has documented medicinal properties**. ABM contains large quantities of beta glucan which has been shown to improve the health of the immune system. It has also been proven to protect against radiation and helps to heal radiation–caused illnesses.
3. **ABM grows**. The relatively short growth cycle means that frequently and continuously a delicious nutraceutical can be produced where it is needed most. Once the infrastructure is in place, a step towards self-sufficiency has begun. Financial resources can be diverted toward other areas.
4. **ABM is economical**. Unlike drugs, mushrooms grow and reproduce. With proper care the crop yield may be expected to grow. Imagine a future in which Africans actually export surplus ABM to waiting world markets.

I would be nicely surprised if you knew about ABM. In Japan 250 companies sell about 500 million dollars worth of ABM a year. ABM and or beta glucan have been used and researched for their effects against cancer and their positive effects on the immune system.

As a well-traveled American, a resident of Japan, a father and an active member of the small-but-growing international ABM community, I offer my resources towards the goal of creating a healthier planet, beginning with the African situation.

Very sincerely,

Stephen Black

blacksteps@hotmail.com

p.s. For much more detailed information, please do an internet search of agaricus blazei murill, beta glucan, the Bioneers and Paul Stamets. I can also send copies of published scientific research supporting any of the claims made in this letter.

AN OPEN LETTER TO DOCTORS

Dear Doctor,

I thank you for your time in reading this with an open mind. My goal is not to convince you why you should consider using ABM, but only to present some of the facts surrounding its usage in Japan.

In Japan ABM is used as a health supplement. There are about 250 companies selling about 500 million dollars worth of it a year. It has been used in Brazil as a native food for centuries, but the industry in Japan began in the '70s, when research papers were presented at established medical, pharmaceutical and oncological conferences.

It is now popularly sold in several forms: dried form, freeze-dried, powdered and liquid extract.

ABM is used by thousands of people as a health supplement.

Some doctors and clinics use ABM as an adjuvant supporting the immune system before, during and after cancer therapies of all kinds. No negative reactions of any type have been reported.

ABM is also being used by many people for its antitumor activities. Research presented to the Japan Cancer Society in 1980 showed that the beta glucan found in ABM is effective against Erlich's ascites carcinoma, sigmoid colonic cancer, ovarian cancer, breast cancer, lung cancer, liver cancer and solid cancer.

Although the Japanese language barrier may be a factor, I have found no major side effects involved with ABM usage. In cases where ABM is being used as a treatment for allergies, there is sometimes a worsening of conditions before the conditions diminish. The high amount of fiber ABM contains may be a consideration for those individuals with recent stomach/intestinal surgery.

Massive over-consumption may result in diarrhea, again because of the fiber content.

ABM is safe for pregnant women.

A polysaccharide called beta glucan is considered (at this point) to be the ingredient in ABM which is most beneficial to the immune system. ABM actually contains several types of beta glucan.

Although there is no U.S. research yet available on ABM beta glucans, a form of beta glucan derived from yeast cells is classified by the FDA as GRAS-Generally Regarded as Safe.

Research on the yeast cell based beta glucan has been conducted by the U.S. Armed Forces Radiobiological Institute, Tulane University School of Medicine and the Harvard Medical School.

The leading cancer treatment in Asia is PSK, which is based largely on polysaccharides found in other mushrooms. It should be noted that although Asians have thousands of years worth of experience with mushrooms, ABM was not introduced into the region until the 1970s. At present, however, there are treatments using ABM extractions being researched and it is my understanding at least one will be on the market by 2004.

Although most of the research available focuses on ABM and cancer, there are numerous pieces of anecdotal information on ABM's successes with hepatitis C, allergies, and atopic dermatitis and auto immune diseases.

As there is a history of clinical ABM usage in the Sao Paolo area of Brazil, I am confident that in that region there exists reliable documentation concerning ABM and AIDS, but again, because of the language barrier (in this case Portuguese) I have not yet been able to find anything but anecdotal information.

It should again be noted that beta glucans are beneficial in minimizing the negative effects of conventional cancer treatments, especially in the case of radiation therapy. (The chapter in this book about beta glucan is recommended reading.)

It should also be noted that in Japan there are hundreds, if not thousands, of cases of anecdotal evidence on ABM's anti-tumor properties. It was the low incidence of immune-system related diseases among the ABM-eating natives of Sao Paolo that lead to the first American research on ABM, written in 1965. At present I can find no evidence of clinical tests being done with ABM.

As with any other food, pesticide levels, contamination and heavy metal content could be issues. The ABM industry is, at present, unregulated. Care should be taken to find an established producer of organic ABM.

This author's intent is to create an awareness of ABM as a food or as a health supplement, though its medical uses are an inherent part of its public perception in Japan. Japan lags behind the U.S. in the testing of drug interaction and I can find no research on how ABM interacts with drugs. Again, however, it has been used as an adjuvant with various chemotherapies in Japan (including radiation therapy) and no negative side effects have been reported.

PLEASE CONTACT ME IMMEDIATELY IF YOU ARE IN A POSITION TO USE ABM IN ANY TYPE OF CLINICAL RESEARCH OR INTERESTED IN USING ABM.

The protein content of ABM is probably the highest of all cultivated mushrooms and ABM also contains many vitamins, minerals, enzymes and amino acids, besides the previously mentioned beta glucans.

Fresh ABM is considered to be a gourmet treat, the dried form can be made into a tea which can be flavored with mint or lemon and it has been my experience that the freeze-dried form is enjoyed by most people, especially those who like mushrooms. Pill forms are also available, but the contents should be studied carefully.

I thank you again for taking the time to read about ABM.

Sincerely,

Stephen Black

blacksteps@hotmail.com

Cancer-Carcinoma of the Breast: Mansell P.W.A., Ichinose H, Reed R.J. Krements E.T. McNamee R.B., DiLuzio N.R., "Macrophage-Mediated Destruction of Human Malignant Cells in Vitro" Journal of National Cancer Institute: 54571-580, 1975

"The initial 9 patients studied had malignant carcinoma of the breast. Control and experimental lesions were injected; subsequent biopsies were performed at varying intervals for histological evaluation. Always when glucan or glucan and RF fraction were administered intralesionally, the size of the lesion was strikingly reduced in a short a period as 5 days...in small lesions; resolution was complete, whereas in large lesions, resolution was partial."

AN OPEN LETTER TO THOSE CONSIDERING ABM FOR THE FIRST TIME

Although you may not have heard of it before, the ABM mushroom is very popular in Japan. Over 250 companies sell about 500 million dollars worth of ABM a year. It is the best-selling health supplement in Japan.

ABM has more protein than almost any other mushroom. It is full of vitamins, minerals, enzymes, amino acids and beta glucans which have been studied for how they help the immune system and their effects against cancer. No side effect has ever been reported and in Japan ABM is used by patients who are also receiving chemotherapy and/or radiation therapy

ABM is related to button mushrooms and portobello mushrooms which are found in most grocery stores and restaurants. Those mushrooms are nutritious and delicious, of course, but they do not contain the chemicals which stimulate the immune system.

As part of a healthy diet, ABM is a delicious way to keep your immune system healthy.

You may be interested in hearing your doctor's opinion on ABM and are strongly suggested to discuss ABM with him or her and how it may benefit your health. There is a letter for doctors in this book that your doctor may like to read.

If you have a question which is not answered in this book, or on our website, www.freezedriedagaricus.com, please write to me at the address on our website and I will do my best to answer your question.

Sincerely,

Stephen Black

Pieces of freeze-dried Agaricus blazei *Murill*.
(photo by Gary Shaw/digital treatment copyright Larry Lough)

One of the many over the counter ABM products. The product shown is a tea.

Miscellaneous notes

Like humans, fungi breathe in oxygen and exhale carbon dioxide.

On a molecular level, mushrooms appear to be more closely related to animals than to plants.

Chitin is the material which makes up the hard part of the cap of ABM. It is the same material that lobster shells are made of.

Mushrooms need to be cooked or treated with acids like lemon juice in order to be digested.

Coke, wine and beer, blue cheese, penicillin, birth control pills and much more all are made possible because of fungi.

To avoid confusion: the popular (and expensive)) gourmet mushrooms called morels are different from Agaricus blazei *Murill*.

Brazil produces about 90 tons of ABM a year.

A producer in Kofu Japan made the news in the spring of 2002 by announcing plans to double production of ABM from 24 tons to 48 tons.
In Germany, 70% of doctors prescribe herbs.

The City of Sao Paolo approved a form of ABM as a treatment for cancer patients in May 1996.

The city of Niihama in Japan has designated ABM as one of its staple products.

The Persian word for garden is paradise.

Bacteria can create a new generation every 30 minutes. Medicines do not. The cells of the immune system, however, can and do improve themselves to be prepared as much as possible for new bacterial generations.

The American Cancer Society estimated that 1,268,000 Americans would be diagnosed with cancer in 2001 and that 1,553,000 people will die of it.

In the United States, one hundred and ten billion dollars is spent annually on treatment and other costs associated with cancer.

Which is more important for good health: food or medicine? Ask your doctor how many hours of nutrition they have studied.

In 2001, Japan Tobacco Inc., the world's third largest tobacco firm signed a deal with biotech companies to market future lung vaccines-cancer vaccines based on stimulating patients' immune systems to destroy cancer.
The deal is with two American companies-the Seattle-based Corixa Corporation and California-based Cell Genesys.

The Freeze-dried Agaricus(FDABM) Homepages

Owner's Room

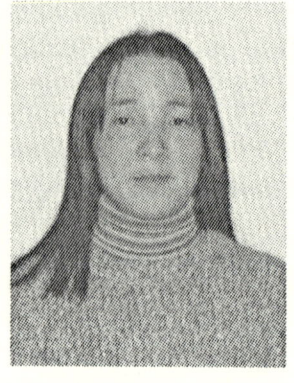

I established this site to increase knowledge about Freeze Dried Agaricus Blasei Murill (FDABM) and to create a forum where FDABM users can share their experiences. I also offer FDABM for sale at a very reasonable price.
My name is Motone Hayakawa. I have a Bachelor's Degree in Pharmacology from Tohoku Pharmacology College and I have been a practicing pharmacologist since 1987. I am also married and have two boys.
I strongly believe ABM is effective and important, especially regarding diseases like cancer, allergies, fatigue, constipation, stiffness and insomnia. It helps prevent colds and is a natural diuretic.
Thank you for visiting and if you have any comments or questions about this site, please do not hesitate to email me. I should mention that I am still studying English so if my response contains a grammatical error I apologize in advance.
Lastly I should mention that ABM is a delicious food and I have included several recipes elsewhere on this site. I wish you good health and look forward to hearing from you.

Sincerely,
Motone Hayakawa

My experiences with FDABM

As a mother of two boys and a licensed pharmacist since 1987, I am always concerned about health issues. I first read about agaricus in 1997. At that time I was interested, but skeptical. I read whatever I could find in newspapers and magazines. Then in 1999,

I had my first agaricus experience. To be honest, I should say that that experience was very unpleasant-the man, a neighbor, died. I found a supplier on the internet and ordered the liquid form. We started giving him the daily portion which we thought would reverse the cancer. It did not.

I cannot say that the supplier sold bad me bad agaricus. I think that man's condition was so far advanced that it may have been impossible to reverse. I still don't know and never will.

I did not give up on ABM, however. In fact, I began to research it even more. I began to think about it more. I have always believed in the healing power of the body, and I have always believed that the body can usually repair itself if it is given the right tools. These tools are the food we eat. Simply, it was during this time that I found out that the only form of agaricus, which can be eaten easily on a daily basis, is the freeze-dried form. This was a big surprise for me.

I thought that if agaricus could be eaten as a regular part of one's diet, this was probably the best. I found out that eating raw agaricus is the most potent form, but the freshness factor makes it difficult to ship and to store. Freeze-dried agaricus (FDABM) seemed to be the ideal way to take agaricus.

It was also during this time that I discovered Taiai. Taiai is the only company that makes freeze-dried ABM. They grow their own and all of their products are made from their own ABM. In Japan they are called the "pioneers of agaricus".

Soon, another test of agaricus presented itself. Another neighbor was found to have a large tumor in his esophagus, so large he couldn't swallow. We started to give him about 4 grams of FDABM mixed in a very thin rice soup. Because it was nearly impossible for him to swallow, he couldn't finish all of the soup in one day. However, he slowly began to improve. About a month later he could swallow easily and he began to gain weight. About three months later he was eating three meals a day. Six months later he was back to riding his bike and the doctor said that monthly visits were no longer necessary.

As he was not taking any other medicine I have no doubt that FDABM was responsible for this recovery.

In the course of my research, I found articles saying that agaricus was also effective against allergies, hepatitis, diabetes and other diseases. It was at this time I decided to tell people about FDABM. My father-in-law had always had severe problems with hay fever. I suggested FDABM to him and he began to take about one gram a day. He began taking FDABM in December 1999 and when the next hay fever season began in February he had no symptoms. That was the first time in twenty years he could breathe easily, without a runny nose and burning eyes.

Up until this I had thought of agaricus as something to fight cancer with. But with my father-in-law's case, it became obvious that FDABM could work with other diseases as well. I decided to try it on myself.

I had had asthma and rhenitis (inflammation of the nasal cavity) since high school. Walking outside was something to be avoided because if I did so, I would cough uncontrollably. Prescribed medicines had serious negative side- effects. After my first son was born the symptoms became stronger. I decided to take 3 grams of FDABM a day. For the first week nothing happened. After that the symptoms worsened. This is considered usual, especially for those with those who take agaricus for allergy relief. Two weeks later the symptoms had disappeared.

When I started taking FDABM, so did my family, mainly as a preventive. I began to serve it in miso soup daily. My husband, who is in good health, had no reactions at all from taking FDABM. Our eldest son had no reactions either. However, the atopic dermatitis of our youngest son went away without his condition worsening.

Fully convinced that FDABM was important not just as a cancer fighter, but powerful against other diseases as well, I set up the Japanese version of this site in October of 2000.

Pets
Pets can get all of the benefits of agaricus that humans can. Because it is almost tasteless, FDABM can be added to most kinds of pet food easily. Most pets like the taste of FDABM.
For the benefits of FDABM against cancer, the recommended

serving is 1 gram for every 15 kilos or 0.0035 oz for every 33 pounds

How to Take/Recipes

FDABM can be eaten straight from the package. One gram is about one tablespoon.
Because it is almost tasteless, FDABM can be added to just about anything. I sometimes eat it with ice cream and there is a restaurant here in Japan that makes sushi with it! Maybe the easiest way is to add it to salads. If you are in a hurry, try mixing it with a little olive oil, a pinch of salt and a dash of your favorite spice.
Following are two soup recipes that my family likes, if you have a favorite FDABM recipe, please let me know and I will post it on the website.

Cream Of ABM Soup

4tbs of sweet butter 2c. of finely chopped onions
1/2c. minced shallots 3c. chicken stock
1 medium size potato peeled and diced 4bunches watercress 1c. heavy cream
12 to 20 grams of FDABM salt, pepper and cayenne to taste

Melt butter in heavy pot. Add onions and shallots and cook covered over low heat until tender. Add chicken stock, potatoes and FDABM, bring to boil. Reduce heat and simmer partially covered until tender, 20 minutes. Remove leaves and tender stems from watercress and rinse. Add watercress, cover, remove from heat and let stand 5 minutes. Pour soup through strainer save reserve liquid and transfer solids to bowl of food processor fitted with steel blade. Add 1 cup cooking stock and process until smooth. Return puree to pot. Stir in heavy cream; add additional stock until desired consistency. Set over medium heat, season to taste with salt, pepper, nutmeg and cayenne.

ABM Miso Soup

5cups of water 3-4tbs of Miso (soy bean paste)
1tbs of instant dashi (Hondashi-bonito soup stock)
3 scallions-chopped 1/2 pkg. of tofu- cut into 1/2 inch squares
12 to 20 grams of FDABM

In a medium sauce pan add 5 cups of water. Bring to a boil, add 1tbs of instant dashi, tofu and FDABM. Reduce heat and simmer about 3 to 5 minutes. Add 1/2 chopped scallions and miso just before end of simmer. Pour soup, top with fresh cut scallions and serve.

FDABM and Beta-glucan

Some of you have written and asked about FDABM and its relationship to beta glucan. For those of you who are not familiar with beta glucan, it is a polysaccharide which has been researched extensively because of its positive effects regarding the immune system and its anticancer/antitumor activities. Note that the word "beta glucan" used in this section refers to beta glucan 1.6/1.3
According to independent tests by the Japan Food Analysis Center in 1998, there were 9 grams of beta glucan per 100 grams of the FDABM tested.(Note however, that only one mushroom was tested, due to cost reasons)
According to independent tests by the Japan Food Research Laboratory, using a different method, there were 16 grams of beta glucan per 100 grams tested.(Again, only one mushroom was tested.)
Even if we use the lower figure of 9 grams, this means that in the suggested daily amount of half a gram of FDABM, there are 45 milligrams of beta glucan 1.3/1.6. If we use the figure supplied by the Japan Food Research Laboratory, the suggested daily amount would contain 80 milligrams.
Ideally, we would like to see more tests done, but at present this has been prohibitively expensive.
Three important things to keep in mind:
1. The figure above is an average based on only two samples. A representative of our supplier told us that since beta glucan is so thoroughly researched that they have made the decision to focus their tests on other, as-yet-unknown components of ABM/FDABM.
2. The two mushrooms tested may be representative of our product's beta glucan level. However, unlike wild agaricus, ours is grown in controlled conditions, which promotes consistency. Our supplier was the first in the world to do this on a large scale. Their growing process is somewhat like growing tomatoes in a greenhouse. Also, please remember that the wild form of ABM is nearly extinct in its native Brazil

due to over-harvesting.
3. As for ABM grown in China or elsewhere, the quality and consistency is variable, dependent upon the grower. ABM/FDABM contains something more than just beta glucans. FDABM also contains vitamins, minerals, enzymes and nucleic acids. Beta glucans by themselves are good for the body, but there is something in ABM which enables it to stimulate the immune system more than beta glucan alone. It is interesting to note that there is a mushroom called meshimakobu which contains more beta glucan than ABM, but which is less effective in its interaction with the immune system.

Again, research on beta glucan is extensive and ongoing. There are a number of technical papers regarding the possibility of an antioxidant unique to ABM which may interact with beta glucan to increase its efficiency.

FDABM FACT SHEET

We believe the freeze-dried form of Agaricus blazei *Murill* is the best form of agaricus to take. Here is why.

Style	Description	Amount	Equivalent amount of raw ABM (grams)	Daily serving (prophylatcic mode)
Freeze-dried Agaricus blazei murill (FDABM)	Large and small pieces, light fragrance	100 grams (2 50 gram pouches)	1000 grams	0.5 grams
Fresh ABM	The real thing	300 grams	300 grams	5 grams
Dried ABM	Dried, hard ABM	100 grams	1000 grams	0.5 grams
Liquid form	30 100cc of liquid in packages	3000cc	600 grams	25cc
Capsule form	200 capsules	500	2 capsules	100
Granule form	Granules; 60 2 gram packages	120 grams	900 grams	0.6 grams

	Advantages	Disadvantages
FDABM	Convenient- can be eaten from the bag or used in cooking	Somewhat bulky
Fresh ABM	Delicious, best source of nutrients	Not easily found
Dried ABM	Least expensive	Must be soaked or made into a tea, usually on a daily basis
Liquid form	Fast- enters the bloodstream quickly. Needs no preparation. Often used in cases where cancer is in an advanced state	Most expensive
Capsule form	Convenient	Difficult to understand the actual amount and source of ABM, may be a mixture
Granule	Convenient	Expensive

*Note: The following equations were used to find the equivalent amount of Raw Agaricus
1 gram of FDABM =10 grams of raw ABM
100cc of liquid ABM extract should=20 grams of raw ABM
The sample package of dried ABM used in this comparison=15 grams raw ABM
The 2 capsules selected for this comparison =5 grams of raw ABM
Numerous studies and experts have agreed that the equivalent of 5 grams of raw ABM, taken on a daily basis, is an effective amount for the prevention of diseases and for maintaining a strong immune system. In cases where diseases are already present, dosages of 30-50 grams of raw agaricus (or the equivalent) are usual.

All of our FDABM is checked by the Japanese government for hygiene. We use only agaricus which we have grown and tested ourselves and have been doing so for over ten years. We are constantly researching and doing all we can to provide you with the highest quality FDABM possible.

The prices, products and amounts are based on a sampling of ABM products found on the internet in March, 2001.

Agaricus blazei *Murill* Components

Vitamins (milligrams per 100 grams)	
Vitamin B1	1.79
Vitamin B2(Riboflavin)	5.20
Pantothenic Acid	2.50
Nicotinic Acid	31.90
Inositol	16.00
Choline	17.00
Vitamin C	86.00
Vitamin D2	5.58
Vitamin K2	5.00

Minerals(mg per 100 grams)	
K2O	55.95
Natrium(Na2 O2)	9.95
Calcium(CaO)	14.95
Fe2O3	2.89
Aluminum (Al2O3)	0.08
Magnesium(MgO)	0.10
Mangan(MnO)	0.04
SO2	2.17
SiO2	1.32
Zinc	1.38
Cobalt	6.50
P2O5	19.23
CO3	9.40
Carium(K)	.84
CuO	.25
Cl	4.38

Nucleic acids
Adenine
Thymine
Cytosine
Guanine

Amino Acids (mg per 100 grams)	
Isoleucine	918
Leucine	484
Lysine	342
Methionine	288
Phenylanine	171
Threonine	234
Tryptophan	406
Valine	652
Aginine	416
Cystine	280
Tyrosine	692
Alanine	350
Aspartic Acid	365
Glutamic Acid	1940
Glycine	224
Proline	362
Serine	234
Histidine	117

Enzymes		
Paokitase	Urease	Lauinase
Esterase	Fenorase	Amegudauase
Lecithinase	Lacase	Rennin
Tannase	PeruokichitaseAsparaginase	
Pectase	Dehidrogenase	Chiroshinase
Sacarase	Sucrase	Chimase
Inperutase	Pekuchinase	Adenirushcurase
Maltase	Decarubokishirase	Okishitase
Toreharase	Interokinase	Lipase
Serurase	Umarase	Arinase
Lactase	Catarase	Lucyarase
Glutamilochitase	Lihenase	Pakimanses
Mannase	Chitase	
Liguninase	Hemisarurase	
Emulicin	Inurase	
Trypsin	Pentozanse	

Research independently conducted by Japanese Food Research Laboratories www.jfrl.or.jp/e/index.html

Kim Z. J. Wang: My experiences with Agaricus blazei Murill

I am a third generation Traditional Chinese Medicine practitioner. In early 2002, I became the first in Hong Kong to begin using Agaricus blazei Murill as a treatment for cancer. The results have been impressive and continuous.

One of the most dramatic recoveries involved an eighty-year old woman who had a case of cancer which had not responded to other forms of treatment, including ling zhi.

Because of my background and experiences, I know that many plants and fungi have healing powers. I also am sadly aware of the fact that there are often unwanted complications surrounding the use of these substances. These complications include: irregularity in quality, irregularity in effectiveness, improper preparation and outright fraud. Also, the natural habitats of many plants and fungi have been poisoned, destroyed or eliminated, meaning to say that the surviving species are usually grown in man-made conditions. This in turn, can result in the use of fertilizers, pesticides and insecticides, which can cause negative reactions in the patient.

In the time that I have been using the freeze-dried form of agaricus, I have not experienced any of these problems. My major problem has been the lack of reliable information in a language besides Japanese. I understand and have seen the large amount of scientific research done on agaricus in Japan and look forward to the time when agaricus is used and studied by people all over the world.

Based in Hong Kong, Kim Zj Wang and his family have developed original successful treatments for many disorders, including insomnia and clinical depression

GLOSSARY

ACTIVATION
The process in which lymphocytes come into contact with antigens and then go into standby until they receive the next chemical signal to expand.

ACTIVE ACQUIRED IMMUNITY
Immunity acquired after the immune system has been sensitized by an antigen. The T and B memory cells remember how the antigen was destroyed the previous time and the next time the antigen appears they use this knowledge to prepare the appropriate defense. This is the theory behind vaccinations.

ADULT STEM CELLS
The cells that build the body but are limited to making one type of tissue. For example, one single human skin stem cell can generate enough cells to cover the entire body.

ADJUVANT
Treatment used in addition to the main treatment. ABM is often used as an adjuvant.

AGARICUS BLAZEI MURILL
A medicinal and gourmet mushroom which is very popular in Japan.

AFFINITY
In regards to the immune system, affinity refers to the tight bond or clinging of an antigen to an antibody bonding site. The tighter the bond is the less chance there is for the antigen to break free. This is important because once an antigen is caught, it cannot cause any harm. The sooner an antibody can neutralize toxins or viruses, the better.
The first time a virus or toxin enters the body, the affinity is weak. However, once the body has memorized the chemical make-up of

the antigen, the affinity will become stronger-as much 1000% stronger! (See also ANTIBODY)

AGARICIN
An antioxidant found in Agaricus blazei *Murill*.

AIDS (Acquired Immune Deficiency Syndrome)
A deficiency of the immune system resulting in the inability to fight disease. The disease is caused by a retrovirus called human immunodeficiency virus (HIV).

ALLERGY
Extreme sensitivity to certain substances such as pollen, food, hair or cloth. Asthma, hay fever, headaches and hives are common symptoms.

ALTERNATIVE MEDICINE
According to the American Cancer Society, alternative therapies are unproven treatments that patients use instead of conventional therapy in an attempt to prevent, lessen or cure disease.
(See also COMPLEMENTARY MEDICINE)

AMINO ACIDS
The building blocks for all protein-based structures in the body. Proteins have the ability to become enzyme or neurotransmitters and function very specifically. The branched chain amino acids are the most important for anabolic support since they are the main molecules involved in the creation of muscle tissue.
There are 22 amino acids in nature. Each of these can be bonded to one another to form short chains called peptides, or long chains called proteins.

ANTHRAX
A disease which forms spores. A single spore has the ability to kill a cow-or a human. There are three types: inhalation anthrax, intestinal anthrax and cutaneous anthrax.

Historically, anthrax was found only in the soil, where it would wait patiently to be released into the air or to be eaten. Once in its victim, the immune system functions as it is supposed to-the spores are detected and then eaten by scavenger cells. The scavenger cells then transport their cargo to the lymph nodes. Usually, in the lymph nodes the cargo is analyzed and appropriate counter measures are prepared.

In the case of anthrax, however, the spores actually want to be eaten. Once inside the scavenger cell, the anthrax spore begins to grow. It assumes its mature form-the anthrax bacterium. Bacteria have the ability to divide and this is exactly what the anthrax does. One becomes two, two becomes four etc. They double their population every half hour. The bacteria also release a poison called Lethal Factor which disrupts the pathway used to send signals to the cell. Once that happens the cell is isolated and can no longer divide. Lethal Factor also weakens the cell walls. The scavenger cell is destroyed and anthrax bacteria are released into the blood stream. Their goal is clear: kill the host and eat it.

It should be noted that low levels of Lethal factor release tumor necrosis factor- the body's own chemotherapy against tumors. There has been some evidence suggesting that DHEA and melatonin may have some effect against the cytokine production caused by anthrax.

Anthrax targets macrophages and forces them to release their anti-inflammatory hormones. Normally inflammation is not such a bad thing- it is a way of treating local infections. Too much of the hormone when released uncontrollably, however, causes septic shock. When this happens, blood vessels leak, blood pressure drops and organs cannot function. The efficiency of the immune system is exploited to help defeat the body as the anthrax multiplies and more macrophages are forced to release more inflammatory hormones. Death occurs and the anthrax feasts. Once the food supply is gone the anthrax bacteria return to their spore form until the cycle can be repeated.

Lethal Factor is in a class of enzymes called protease. In developing treatments for HIV, scientists have come up with drugs called protease inhibitors. Since1996 protease inhibitors, combined with other drugs, have enabled many AIDS patients to improve their health to some degree. With this in mind, it seems similar treatments for anthrax could possibly be developed.

There is also a relationship between certain types of cancer and anthrax. The same pathway that is turned off by Lethal Factor is turned on in some cancer cells, causing the cancer cell to multiply uncontrollably. The more this pathway is studied, the more we can learn to treat both diseases.

Cipro, the main treatment at present, is a synthetic microbial agent. The side effects include vomiting, diarrhea, headaches, dizziness, sun sensitivity and rash.

ANTIBODY

Also called immunoglobulins, antibodies are produced by white blood cells called B cells (or B lymphocytes). They are glycoproteins which bind or catch viruses and toxins very effectively. The strength of this bond is referred to as affinity.

In human there are five types of antibodies: IgG, IgA, IgM, IgD and IgE. Each of these antibodies is specialized and located in a different section of the immune system.

(See also ANTIGEN, B Cells, IgG, IgA, IgM, IgD, IgE)

ANTIGEN

Any substance of a biological nature which, when it enters the body, causes the production of antibodies. The bits of proteins found on the surface of cancer cells function as antigens, which makes them potential targets for destruction by the immune system. There are at least twenty antigens.

The three chemical classes of antigens are proteins, sugars (complex carbohydrates), and fats. The higher the molecular weight, the bigger the immune system reaction is.

ANTIGEN PRESENTING CELLS

There are two groups of antigen presenting cells in the body: those which move and those which do not. The mobile ones, like

macrophages, patrol the bloodstream and bodily fluids, while the other group, dendritic cells, are anchored in tissue.
Once these cells have discovered antigens, they present this information to the supervisory parts of the immune system.

ANTIOXIDANT
compounds like vitamin C, vitamin E and beta carotene which block chemical reactions with oxygen and reported to reduce the risk of cancer.

APOPTOSIS
A naturally occurring process in which the cell commits suicide. Normally, this occurs after a certain number of cell divisions or when the cell detects damage to its DNA. Tumors start to grow quickly once they can eliminate their apoptosis programming. Though damaged, they continue to live and divide.

ARGININE
An amino acid, arginine has been studied for its beneficial effects on the immune system, the kidneyss and the blood, as well as its indirect stimulation of growth hormone release and its ability to affect nitric oxide levels in the blood.
A diet high in the amino acid lysine and low in arginine has become a regular treatment for herpes.
ABM has about 416 milligrams of arginine per 100 grams.

ARTHRITIS
A disease of the immune system, in which it mistakenly attacks the connective tissue and cushioning joints of the body.(see also AUTO-IMMUNE DISEASE)

AUTO-IMMUNE DISEASE
The term used when the body mistakenly begins to attack itself. Crohn disease, lupus, rheumatoid arthritis, hepatitis, ulcerative colitis, multiple sclerosis and allergies are all autoimmune diseases.

B CELLS
B cells are special types of white blood cells which produce antibodies and which are produced in great numbers, each with the ability to recognize one of the millions of microbial antigens in our environment. Once a foreign antigen is recognized by a B cell, it multiplies and changes into an antibody factory-a plasma cell.
The huge numbers of B cells and the fact that only a small percentage of them will ever encounter the antigen they are sensitive to my seem like unnecessary overproduction is actually a safety precaution as we are prepared for all possible antigens, whether we encounter them or not.
Before birth, B cells are produce by the liver. After birth, they are produced in the marrow. B cells were discovered in the 1950s.

BASOPHIL
A cell that produces chemicals such as histamine. Basophils are responsible for some allergic reactions. Less than 1% of all white blood cells are basophils.

BETA GLUCAN
A sugar molecule (a polysaccharide) that has been studied and used for its effects on the immune system.

CANCER
A cell that has lost the ability to control its division and has divided so much that it has become a growth which feeds from the body.

COMPLEMENT
The division of the immune system that is composed of heat-sensitive proteins and their biologically active components which cause the breakdown and destruction of antibody-coated cells

COMPLEMENTARY MEDICINE
According to the National Cancer Society, complementary

medicines are those used along with conventional medicine. Also, according to the NCS, "many of these therapies have been shown to help relieve symptoms and improve quality of life by lessening the side effects of conventional treatments or providing psychological and physical benefits to the patient".

CYCLOSPORIN
A billion-dollar drug derived from a fungus which uses insects as its host

CYTOKINES
Chemical messengers that allow cells in the immune system to communicate.

EOSINOPHILS
Cells that have the ability to eat antibody complexes

FEVER
The increase in body temperature which is a defense against infection.

FUNGI
Those members of the plant family which live by breaking own and absorbing the organic materials in which they grow. Includes mushrooms, molds, mildews, smuts, rusts and yeasts.

GRIFON
The trademarked name for a maitake extract

HELPER T CELL
A lymphocyte that detects foreign proteins and initiates antibody production.

HIMEMATSUTAKE
One of the Japanese names for ABM. It translates as "princess mushroom".

I.P
Intraperitoneally; injected into the peritoneum of the abdominal cavity

IgA
The antibody found in mucous.

IgD
The antibody which functions mainly as as antigen receptor on B cells.

IgE
The antibody involved in most allergic reaction.

IgG
The most abundant immunoglobulin in the blood. It provides most of the immunity against infections which could occur in the blood.

IgM
The first antibody produced in an immune response. It quickly identifies the invader while the other defense mechanisms catch up.

IMMUNE SYSTEM
The chemicals, cells, tissues and organs involved in keeping the body immune from disease.

IMMUNOGLOBULIN
See ANTIBODY

INFLAMMATION
Swelling, redness, and pain associated with injuries and infections. The three stages are heat, swelling, reddening and pain/

INTEGRATIVE MEDICINE-

Emphasizes the restoration of health rather than just disease treatment and aims to restore confidence in the body's ability to heal itself.

INTERFERONS
Proteins which occur naturally in the body and have been shown to have anti-viral, anti-inflammatory and anti-scarring properties.

INTERLEUKINS
Critical for the growth, mobility and differentiation of lymphoid and other cells. They are produced by leukocytes.

K-2
An alpha glucan molecule found in ABM, cordyceps, sinemsis and other mushrooms

KANPO
The Japanese word for traditional Chinese medicine

KAWARIHARATAKE
Another Japanese name for ABM.

KILLER T CELLS
The assassins of the immune system, they are based in the lymph nodes where they wait for macrophages to bring in antigens. Once this happens, they begin to divide immediately and rush out through the blood stream to seek out and kill the diseased cell. They are sometimes called CD8 cells because that is one of the proteins they have on their surface.

KRESTIN
Krestin or PSK is an anticancer drug which was developed in 1975. It is a derivative of the mushroom called coriolus versicolor and has also proven to be an anti-viral agent.

L-ARGININE

An amino acid that is essential for muscle growth and tissue repair. Studies have shown that use of arginine (as it is also called) can improve immune responses to bacteria, viruses and tumor cells. It also promotes wound healing and regeneration of the liver.

L.E.M.
Stands for Lentinula edodes mycelia, an extract from shiitake which has been shown to have anti-tumor and antiviral activity

LENTINAN
Was licensed by the Japanese government as a treatment for cancer in 1985. It is made from the shiitake mushroom.

LENTINULA EDODES
Scientific name for the reishi fungus, also called ling zhi

LIVER
The largest organ in the body, it affects nearly every metabolic process in the body, either directly or indirectly.

LYMPH
The clear fluid that surrounds all body cells and carries immune cells.

LYMPH NODES
Nodules in the neck, groin and, abdomen and armpits that develop and store white blood cells and also filter disease-causing organisms out of the lymph system.

LYMPHOKINES
Secreted by T-cells, these chemical messengersencourage cell growth and direct cellulr traffic. They also destroy cells and activate macrophages.

LYSINE
An amino acid from which carnitine is synthesized. It is important

because it is responsible for the energy producing units in the mitochondria.

MACROPHAGE
A cell in the immune system which has the ability to eat and digest bacteria and viruses. Macrophages also eat cellular debris. All of this information they then display on their surface so that the identity of the intruders may be passed on to the rest of the immune system.

MAITAKE
A very popular Japanese gourmet and medicinal mushroom that is known for its anti-cancer properties.

MYCELIUM
The network of cells which form the vegetative part of the fungus.

MYCORRHIZAL
A term used to describe the relationship between a plant or tree and fungi. Usually in this type of relationship the fungus breaks down organic matter which makes nutrients more available for the plant.

NATIONAL FOUNDATION FOR ALTERNATIVE MEDICINE
The organization set up by former Congressman Berkley Bedell that monitors clinics and doctors who are using alternative treatments for disease.

NATURAL KILLER CELLS
Have the ability to kill certain organisms and cells without any guidance from the rest of the immune system.

NEUTROPHIL
A killer cell which eats intruding bacteria and viruses. More than half of the total white blood cells are neutrophils.

NITRIC OXIDE

Can be created from L-arginine by the enzyme nitric oxide synthase. It has been studied for its role as a communicator between cells. Conversion of arginine to NO has been shown to have anti-aging benefits in addition to the ability to dilate the blood vessels, increase circulation and may positively affect male and female potency.

PEMPHIGUS
Refers to those skin diseases that involve the immune system.

PEPTIDE
A short chain of amino acids

PHYTOCHEMICALS
Chemical compounds produced by plants. They are found in grains, vegetables, fruits, plants, mushrooms and other fungi. Thousands have been identified, but only a few have been studied closely. Beta carotine, beta glucan, vitamin C and vitamin E are examples of phytochemicals.
Some may have no nutritional value but still are able to influence the body.

POLYSACHARIDES
The name given to large, complex sugar molecules.

PROTEASE
A class of enzymes that negatively affect the body. Protease inhibiting drugs have been developed to fight HIV.

PROTEIN
Long chains of amino acids

PSK
See Kreskin

PSORIASIS
An autoimmune disease in which the skin becomes unusually thick

and full of very large numbers of killer T cells.

REISHI
A mushroom called the herb of immortality by the Chinese. It has a free radical scavenging effect and prevents oxidative damage. It is excellent for the liver.

RETICULOENDOTHILIAL SYSTEM (RES)
That part of the immune system which is made up of highly phagocytic cells. This system protects against microbial infection and is responsible for the removal of worn-out blood cells.

SCHIZOPHYLLAN-licensed by the Japanese government as an immunostimulant therapy for cancer

SELF VS. NONSELF
The guiding principle of the immune system. Viruses, bacteria, worms and microbes are not part of the body- non-self- and are identified by the body as quickly as possible so that they can be destroyed as quickly as possible. Transplanted organs are also classified as non-self which is why rejection of the transplant is an issue. Tumors have or create many of the same characteristics as self, which is why the body cannot immediately recognize and destroy them.

SHIITAKE
A popular and delicious mushroom sold throughout Japan in grocery stores. It contains beta-glucan and an anti-tumor medicine called Lentinan is derived from it.

SPORE
Reproductive cells of fungi

SPOROPHORE
The fruit body of a mushroom

STRESS
Proven to negatively effect the immune system and decreases the ability to fight cancer and viruses. Also accelerates the aging process.

TCM
Traditional Chinese Medicine. The use of herbs, fungi and plants as medicinal treatments. The first written records of TCM are from 100 B.C.

TRYPTOPHAN-niacin
Synthesized from the essential amino acid tryptophan. Tryptophan can also be converted to the important neurotransmitter serotonin. It has been studied for its role in inducing sleep.

THYMUS
Nearly covering the chest area in children, the thymus shrinks after It is where the T-4 cells, the brains of the immune system, are programmed to fight disease.

TUMOR
An abnormal mass of tissue which can be benign (not cancerous) or malignan (cancerous).

TUMOR NECROSIS FACTOR
A molecule produced by macrophages to kill tumors

Bibliography

Agaricus Popularity Continues, Kenkou Sangyo Shibun (Health Industry Newspaper), January 4, 2001

Brynie, Faith Hickman, 101 Questions About Your Immune System You Felt Defenseless to Answer...Until Now, Twenty-First Century Books, A Division of the Millbrook Press, Inc. 2000

Cell Biology and Toxicology, 2000, Vol 16, Iss 3, pp 165-174, printed in Life Extension, May 2001, pg 79

Chen J, Wollman Y, Chernichovsky T, Iaina A, Sofer M, Matzkin H. Effect of oral administration of high-dose nitric oxide donor L-arginine in men with organic erectiledysfunction: results of a double-blind, randomized, placebo-controlled study. BJU Int 1999 Feb;83(3):269-73

Clancy John Jr., Basic concepts in immunology: a student's survival guide, McGraw Hill, 1998

Desowitz Robert, The Thorn in the Starfish, W.W. Norton & Company, 1987, New York

Dwyer, John M., The body at war: the miracle of the immune system, NAL Penguin Inc, 1989 New York

Edelson, Edward, The Immune System, Chelsea House Publishers,

Gabor, Somlyai, Let's Defeat cancer! The biological effect of deuterium depletion, akemai kiado, 2000 Budapest

Gordon GB, Shantz LM, Talay P. Modulation of growth, differentiation and carcinogenesis by dehydropiandrosterone. Adv Enzyme Regul.1987; 26:355-382

Gutnik,Martin J. , Immunology: from Pasteur to the search for an AIDS vaccine, A Venture book, 1989

Hall, Stephen S. A commotion in the blood:life, death and the immune system, Henry Holt and Co., New York, 1997

Hasegawa T, Okunda M,Nomoto K, Yoshikai Y. Augmentation of resistance against Listeria monocytogenes by oral administration of a hot water extract of Chlorella vulgaris in mice. Immunopharmacol Immunotxicol 1994; May; 16(2);191-202

Herbert J. Neurosteroids, brain damage and mertal illness. Exp Gerontol 1998 Nov-Dec, 33(7-8):713-27

Higaki M, Eguchi F, Watanabe Y, A stable culturing method and pharmacological effects of the Agaricus Blazei, Nippon Yakurigaki Zasshi 1997 Oct;110 Suppl 1:98P-103P

Hobbs, Christopher, L. Ac., Medicinal Mushrooms: An Exploration of Tradition, Healing and Culture, Botanica Press, Second Edition, February, 1995, Santa Cruz, California

Hseu,Ruey-Syang PhD(National Taiwan Industry), "Lingzhi vs. Immune System & Liver Functions", Lecture, Suntex Singapore International Convention Center, October 13, 2002

Ikekawa.T et al. 1969. Antitumor activity of aqueous extracts of edible mushrooms. *Cancer Research* 29:734-735

Ito H, Shimura K, Itoh H, Kawade M, Antitumor effects of a new polysaccharide-protein complex(ATOM) prepared from Agaricus blazei (Iwade strain 101)îHimematsutakeî and its mechanisms in tumor-bearing mice , Anticancer Research 1997 Jan-Feb(1A9:227-84

Itoh H, Itoh H, Amano H, Noda H, Inhibitory action of a (1-->6)-beta-D glucan-protein complex (III-2-b) isolated from Agaricus blazei Murill (ihimematsutakeî) on Meth A fibrosarcoma-bearing mice and its antitumor mechanism, Japan Journal of Pharmacology 1994 October;66(2):265-71

Kakuta, Mariko, Kaku Hanae, Misaki, Akira Some properties of Beta galactose-binding Letin Isolated from Fruiting Body of Agaricus Blazei ,Journal of Molecular Nutrition(Japanese title:Biryo Eisyo Kenkyu) pg 111-117, 1999

Kakuta, Mariko, Tanigawa Akiko, Kikuzaki Hiroe, Misaki, Akira, Isolationa and Chemical Characterization of Antioxidative Substance and Glucans from fruiting body of Agaricus Blazei,Journal of Molecular Nutrition(Japanese title: Biryo Eiyoso Kenkyu), pg 83-90,2000

Kim HS, Kacew S, Lee BM. In vitro chemopreventative effects of plant polysaccharides (Aloe barbadensis Miller, Lentius edodes, Ganoderma lucidum and Coriolis Versicolor). Carcinogenesis 1999 Aug;20(8):1637-1640

Koff WC, Dunegan MA. Modulation of macrophage-mediated tumoricidal activity by neuroppeptides and neurohormones. J Immunol 1985 Jul;135(1):350-4

Lappeí, Marc, The Tao of Immunology: A revolutionary new understanding of our bodyís defenses, Plenum Publishing, New York, 1997

Lee CK, Han SS, Shin YK, Chung MH, Park YI, Lee SK, Kim YS. Prevention of ultraviolet radiation-induced suppression of contact hypersensitivity by Aloe vera gel components. Intl J Immunopharmacol 199 May;21(5):303-10

Lin JJ, Cybulsky AV, Goodyer PR, Fine RN, Kaskel FJ. Insulin-like growth factor-1 enhances epidermal growth factor receptor activation and renal tube cell regeneration in postischematic acute renal failure. J Lab Clin Med 1995 Jun;125(6):724-33

Lydard, P.M.,Whelan A., Fanger M.W., Instant Notes in Immunology, Bios Springer
Mycelial Magic:the Fungal restoration, presentation by paul Stamets, The Bioneers Conference, San Rafael california,2001

Mizuno M, Morimoto M, Minato K, Tsuchida H, Polysaccharides from Agaricus Blazei stimulate lymphocyte T-cells subsets in mice, Bioscience Biotechnology and Biochemistry 1998 March, 62(3):434-7

Mizuno Takahashi, Hagiwara Toshihiko,Nakamura Takuji, Ito, Hoshino, Shimura Keishiro, Toshimitsu Sumiya,Asakura Akihiro, Antitumor Activity and Some Properties of Water-soluble Polysaccharides from Himematsutake, the Fruiting Body of Agaricus blazei Murill Agricultural Biological Chemistry.,54 (11), 2889-2896,1990

Misaki, Akira,Kakuta, Mariko, Fungal(1-39-Beta D Glucans:Chemistry and Antitumor Activity, Carbohydrates in Drug Design, Marcel Dekker, Inc. New York 1997

Mizuno Takashi, Ando Motoharu, Sugie Reiko, Ito Hitoshi, Shimura Keishiro, Sumiya Toshimitsu, and Matsuura Akira , Antitumor Activity of Some Polysaccharides Isolated From an Edible Mushroom, *Ningyotake,* the Fruiting Body and the Cultured Mycelium of *Polyporous confluens* Bioscience, Biotechnology, Biochemistry, 56(1),34-41,1992

Osaki Y, Kato T, Yamamoto K, Okubo J, Miyazaki T, Antimutagenic and bactericidial substances in the fruit body of a Basidiomycete Agaricus blazei, Jun-17 Yakugaku Zasshi 1994 May 114(5):342-50

Nilsson Lennart, The Body Victorious, Delacorte Press, New York

Mizuno Takahashi, Mushrooms: The Versatile Fungus Food and Medicinal Properties, Food Reviews International Volume 11, Number 1,(167-172)Marcel Dekker, Inc. New York, Basel, Hong Kong 1995

Andrew Pollack, International Herald Tribune, Down on the Pharm, Dream of Drugs from Milk Begins to Fade Business/Finance Section November 24-25, 2001

Roberts E. The importance of dehydroepiandrosterone sulfate(in the blood of primates): a longer and healthier life? Biochem Pharmacol 1999 Feb 15;57(4):329-46

Robbins, Anthony. Anthony Robbins' PowerTalk, Volume 22, audiocassette featuring an interview with Dr. Deepak Chopra, Guthy-Renker

Song L, Wang D, Cui X, Hu W. The protective action of taurine and L-arginine in radiation pulmonary fibrosis. J Environ Pathol Toxicol Oncol 1998;17(2): 151-7

Stamets, Paul, Growing Gourmet and Medicinal Mushrooms (Third Edition) 1993, 2000 Ten Speed Press, Berkley California.

Tanaka K, Yamada A et al. A novel glycoprotein obtained from Chlorella shows antimetastatic immunopotentiation. Cancer Immunol Immunother 1998; Feb 45(6):213-20

Teo Pau Lin, The Politics of Mushrooms, The Straits Times, October 20, 2002

Nicholas Wade, International Herald Tribune, In Stem Cells, Glimpses of the Body's Master Plan, December 20, 2001

Nicholas Wade, International Herald Tribune, The Quest for Everlasting Health, December 20, 2001

Index

Agaricus blazei *Murill* 12,35,36,39,43,46,49,50,51-80
benefits 34
history 13-18
photos of growth cycle 21
recipes 70,71
sales figures 14
sushi 26
tempura 29
tea 49
varieties 53
Adjuvant 54
AIDS 12,13,58
Allergies 57
Anecdotes 14
Anti-aging 36
Anti-oxidant 36
Arthritis 42
Asthma 42
Autoimmune diseases 42
Aptosis 46
Beta glucan 16,31,32,36-39,50,54,55,57,58,60,61,72,73
Bono 55
Bioneers 10
CNN 7
Coca Cola 20
Cancer 47-48
Chitin 64
Dermatitis 42-50
Diabetes 42
Dorsey, Dr. Larry 10
Fiber 31,35
Freeze-dried agaricus 8
Photo,freezedried ABM 62
Freeze Dried ABM Center 7

Fybromalgia 42
Gates, Bill 55
Hamaichi restaurant 27
Hayakawa,Motone 13,14, 66
Hepatitis C 50
Himematsutake 11
HIV 12,13,58
Homeostasis 42
Ikegawa, Dr.16
Immune System 41,42,48
Immunity 41
Interleukins 46
Japan Cancer Society 16,57
Lambert, Dr. E.D.16
Low Dog, Dr.Tieraona 10
Lymphokines 46
Macrophages 37,46
Maitake 19
Mie Prefecture 16
Multiple sclerosis 42
Murrill,William 13,15
Mycellia 23
Natural Killer (NK) cells 37,46
People magazine 7
Pets 68
Piedade 16
Polysaccharides-see beta glucan
PSK 19,58
Radiation, 36,38
Reishi 43
Rheumatism 50
Rhenitis 68
Sao Paolo 16,23,58,64
Shibata Shoji 16
Shiitake 19,43
Sinden, W.J. 16

South China Morning Post 7
Stamets, Paul 10,14,24,32,55,56
Taiai 7,67
Tokyo University 16,43
Tumor 47,48
Tumor Necrosis Factor 46
Turkey tail 19,43
United States Armed Forces Radiobiological Institute 36,58
University of California at Los Angeles 37
Weil, Dr .Andrew 10,24,32
Yahoo 17